Inv
and
Renfrewshire
40 favourite Walks

The author and publisher have made every effort to ensure that the information in this publication is accurate, and accept no responsibility whatsoever for any loss, injury or inconvenience experienced by any person or persons whilst using this book.

published by
pocket mountains ltd
The Old Church, Annanside,
Moffat DG10 9HB

ISBN: 978-1-907025-822

Text and photography copyright © Keith Fergus 2022

The right of Keith Fergus to be identified as the Author of this work has been asserted by him in accordance with the Copyright, Designs and Patents Act 1988

A catalogue record for this book is available from the British Library

Contains Ordnance Survey data © Crown copyright and database 2022 supported by out of copyright mapping 1945-1961

Printed in Poland

Introduction

The regions of East Renfrewshire, Renfrewshire and Inverclyde lie at the western edge of Scotland's Central Belt, bordered by Glasgow, Lanarkshire and Ayrshire. These three regions have much in common, by way of both industrial heritage and landscape, and their natural assets – the rivers, the moorland and the coastline – have in recent centuries been pivotal in enabling towns and villages to grow and prosper here. Today, it's these same natural assets that make walking here so rewarding.

With far-reaching views around almost every corner, there's also much to be learned about the industrial heritage of these areas while out exploring. There is evidence of Roman occupation in and around Paisley (the Romans named it *Vanduara*) while there are traces left by Iron Age inhabitants in Busby and on the summit of Duncarnock above Neilston. Paisley Abbey was established during the 12th century and it became an important commercial centre for trade across Europe, with great influence and wealth following.

Within East Renfrewshire and Renfrewshire, rivers such as the Levern Water, the Gryffe and the White Cart Water were all central to the thread, cotton and textile industries in Neilston, Barrhead, Houston, Eaglesham, Kilbarchan and Paisley from the 18th century. Paisley, in particular, became a textile giant, with a peerless weaving heritage, and the town is known across the globe for its famous Paisley Pattern. Although its teardrop motif had its origins in Persia, Paisley adopted the design during the 19th century, particularly in its cotton and silk Paisley shawls. The Coats and Clark families were instrumental in making Paisley the centre of the thread and cotton industries.

Away from Paisley and a 5km stretch of the Levern Water, between Barrhead and Neilston, was home to several cottonmills. The biggest was Neilston's Crofthead Mill, which first opened in 1792 and at its height employed around 1500 people. Another 1000 worked in the nearby bleachfields and calico printing works. Many of these workers were local people but many more were immigrants from Ireland and the North and West Highlands of Scotland, meaning the village grew substantially. Crosslee Cotton Mill, near Houston, was the largest mill on the River Gryffe, having opened in 1793, and in its heyday employed upwards of 300 workers. Eaglesham had two mills, employing more than 200 people, while Kilbarchan once had an extraordinary 800 handlooms within the village.

Heading out to the coast, shipbuilding was the dominant industry from the 1700s, with Greenock and Port Glasgow second only to Glasgow as centres for shipbuilding. The River Clyde has been key to the industry of Greenock – by the early 1600s, a pier had been built on the river and the town quickly established itself as an important port. After the 1707 Act of Union it became the main port for the West Indies, and one of the Clyde's most famous yards, Scotts, was established in Greenock in 1711 where ships were built for 277 years. The first yard in Port Glasgow, Thomas McGills, opened in 1780, and it too became a centre for shipbuilding. Port Glasgow was also where *The Comet*, the first commercial steam vessel in Europe, was built in 1812.

As well as shipbuilding, sugar refining played a prominent role in Greenock's prosperity during the 1800s with 14 refineries processing sugar from the Caribbean. The historic affluence of the town dubbed 'Sugaropolis' is linked, inextricably, with the slave trade, as it is in Port Glasgow. Reflecting the wealth of a period when many of the town's civic leaders were merchants involved in the slave economy in a variety of ways are some of Greenock's most imposing buildings, including Custom House and Victoria Tower.

The natural environment
The landscape of East Renfrewshire, Renfrewshire and Inverclyde would generally be described as rolling with a number of high points, including Duncarnock above Barrhead, Windy Hill in Muirshiel Country Park, and much of the high ground of Clyde Muirshiel Regional Park, having widespread and extensive views across much of Central and Southern Scotland.

Although the routes described in this guide span the western edge of Scotland's heavily populated Central Belt, meaning you are never far from human habitation, the plants and wildlife that can be seen on these walks is surprising.

Dolphins, porpoise and even orcas can be spotted at times in the Firth of Clyde. Oystercatcher, redshank, common guillemot, red-breasted merganser, red-throated diver and great black-backed and black-headed gulls may also be seen along the coast.

At the other end of the scale, butterflies, dragonflies and damselflies thrive out on the moorland of Clyde Muirshiel Regional Park, Eaglesham Moor and Gleniffer Braes while wildflowers line woodland and countryside paths criss-crossing all three regions; the carpets of bluebells found in the Bluebell and Rannoch Woods of Johnstone and snowdrops in Finlayston Country Estate and Ardgowan Estate are particularly special.

The countryside and moorland is also home to a variety of birdlife, such as lapwing, skylark, hen harrier and buzzard while the many dams and lochs dotted across the landscape are ideal sites for spotting geese, great crested grebes, tufted ducks, goldeneye, goosander, mute swans and black-headed gulls.

How to use this guide

The 40 walks within this guidebook are between 1.5km and 12km in length and can be completed within half a day. The region has good public transport links across Scotland's Central Belt and the majority of the walks are accessible by bus or train (travelinescotland.com).

Most of these walks are low level and make use of the excellent network of paths. A few are child friendly and any rocky, boggy or steep terrain is highlighted at the start of each route. It is not advisable to stray from the described walks onto farmland or near exposed cliffs, and where livestock is present dogs must be kept on leads.

Some routes cross steep hill or moorland terrain where good map-reading and navigational skills are necessary in poor weather. Winter walking brings distinct challenges, particularly the limited daylight hours, whilst strong winds, especially along the coast and over higher ground, are possible throughout the year.

Even in summer, warm waterproof clothing is advisable and footwear that is comfortable and supportive with good grips is a must. Don't underestimate how much food and water you need and remember to take any medication required, including reserves in case of illness or delay. Do not rely on receiving a mobile phone signal when out walking.

Each route begins with an introduction summarising the terrain walked, the distance covered, the average time to walk the route and the relevant Ordnance Survey (OS) map.

There is a route for almost all levels of fitness in this guide, but it is important to know your limitations. Even for an experienced walker, colds, aches and pains can turn an easy walk into an ordeal.

Access

Until the Land Reform (Scotland) Act was introduced in 2003, the 'right to roam' in Scotland was a result of continued negotiations between government bodies, interest groups and landowners. In many respects, the Act simply reinforces the strong tradition of public access to the countryside of Scotland for recreational purposes. However, a key difference is that under the Act the right of access depends on whether it is exercised responsibly.

Landowners also have an obligation not to unreasonably prevent or deter those seeking access. The responsibilities of the public and land managers are set out in the Scottish Outdoor Access Code (outdooraccess-scotland.scot).

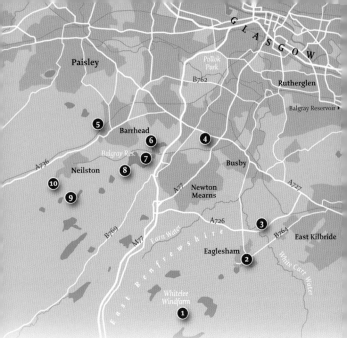

East Renfrewshire is a great place to walk, taking in fabulous scenery, history and wildlife. It has a history that extends back many thousands of years, an example of which is the remains of the ancient fort on the top of Duncarnock on the outskirts of Neilston. Nearby, the summit of Neilston Pad has a panorama across much of Glasgow and Renfrewshire to Arran and the Southern Highlands. Fereneze Braes above Barrhead is another fine vantage point.

Milling is at the heart of East Renfrewshire's industrial heritage, and this is evident when walking through Neilston and Eaglesham. The focal point,

meanwhile, of a foray into Dams to Darnley Country Park, on the outskirts of Barrhead, is its reservoirs: the variety of wildlife that can be spotted when walking here is hard to beat.

Further east, a network of paths weave through Rouken Glen Park (voted the UK's Best Park in 2016), across peaceful parkland, along riverbanks and within its wooded confines.

Whitelee Windfarm highlights that engineering accomplishments on a vast scale are not a thing of the past and it is a site that has opened up the surrounding moorland, with more than 130km of paths and tracks and sweeping views to enjoy.

East Renfrewshire

Whitelee Windfarm

Distance 11.25km Time 3 hours 30
Terrain tracks and paths
Map OS Explorer 334 Access no public
transport to the start

Whitelee Windfarm, a few miles southwest of Eaglesham, is the largest onshore windfarm in Britain and the second largest in Europe. As well as more than 200 turbines spread across Eaglesham Moor, there's over 130km of paths and tracks, making this a great place to walk or mountain bike.

The walk begins from the car park for the seasonal Whitelee Windfarm Visitor Centre, home to an excellent exhibition and café. Leaving the car park, return to the access road and turn right to go around a barrier. This track drops, then rises to a junction. Turn left and continue for 300m to meet a path for 'Lochgoin'.

Turn right onto this, ignoring the immediate branch to the left for the bike trails. At the next junction, turn left and, after another 150m, go right. Turning left at the end, a track descends over a cattle grid and into a wilder section of moor, with Lochgoin Reservoir coming into view. Keep an eye out for skylark, lapwing, buzzard, kestrel and even hen harrier. The moor is also home to tawny, short-eared and barn owls. From here, the view extends across Dunwan Dam and Glasgow to the rolling barrier of the Campsie Fells. On a clear day Stob Binnein and Ben More above Crianlarich may be visible. The prominent outline of Dunwan Hill can be seen nearby, with the remains of a fort on its summit.

Easy walking continues across Eaglesham Moor as you make a broad loop around the west end of Lochgoin Reservoir, ignoring any paths branching off to the left. The track is lined with many species of lichen, and in summer small heath butterflies and six-spot Burnet moths flit amongst the grasses.

◂ Turbines of Whitelee Windfarm

In 4km or so, the route gains a track on the right, again signposted for Lochgoin. Follow this down towards the southern shore of the reservoir, with a view of Arran's serrated contours on the horizon. Upon reaching the reservoir itself follow a path across a grassy embankment. It is a lovely spot for a break, with views across the moor.

Nearby, to the southwest, is Lochgoin Farm and, on the horizon, the Lochgoin Monument, which was erected in 1896 in memory of John Howie of Lochgoin, a biographer best known for *The Scots Worthies*, a collection of potted biographies of Scottish Protestant heroes through the ages. The farmhouse was a noted refuge for Covenanters in the 17th century and it is probable that illegal Conventicles, or assemblies, were held on Eaglesham Moor during what became known as 'the Killing Time'.

At the head of Lochgoin Reservoir, cross a bridge and go through a gate and the Eaglesham Angling Association's car park. After another gate, follow a track to reach a windfarm access road. Turn right and continue for 700m to reach a track on the right. This takes you northeast across the moor on the north side of Lochgoin Reservoir for 1.5km to rejoin the outward route at the junction just before the cattle grid. Turn left here, keeping left, then turning right to soon pass the MTB trails, with fine views as you retrace your steps to the start.

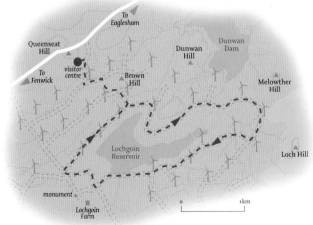

Eaglesham Heritage Trail

Distance 1.5km Time 1 hour
Terrain woodland and parkland paths,
pavement Map OS Explorer 334
Access buses to Eaglesham from Glasgow

Eaglesham was named as Scotland's
first conservation village in 1960 and
is a fascinating place to wander around.
The planned village was the vision of
Alexander Montgomery – the 10th Earl of
Eglinton – who replaced the medieval
settlement of Kirkton with Eaglesham in
1769. It was built around Polnoon Street,
Montgomery Street and Mid Road, giving
Eaglesham its classic 'A'-shaped design.

The route begins from the corner of
Gilmour Street and Polnoon Street in
Eaglesham village centre. Here stands the
impressive Polnoon Lodge, which was
built as a hunting lodge in 1733 by the
Montgomery Family and has over the
years served as a temperance hotel,
boarding house and care home.

Cross Gilmour Street onto Polnoon
Street, then immediately turn left onto
a path that runs along the The Orry – an
area of common ground – towards the
Eglinton Arms Hotel.

At a crossroads, turn right and climb a
path west through The Orry all the way
to Mid Road. Turn right to reach Polnoon
Street, and right again to walk the short
distance to St Bridget's Church, which sits
just back from the road. It was founded
in 1858 and named after St Bridget
(or St Bride) who was born in 451 in
Dunkald in Ireland.

Walk back along Mid Road, cross a
bridge over a burn, turn right and
continue up through The Orry – the
village green where the New Orry Cotton
Mill was located. The mill began
production in 1791 and at its peak
employed 200 people over an impressive
five floors. It was the village's main
employer for more than 70 years but was
badly damaged by fire in 1831 and again in
1876, after which it closed.

◄ The Orry

Continue to Polnoon Street, turn left, follow the pavement for 75m, then turn left back into The Orry. Fork right to follow a path rising into a pocket of woodland, the colours spectacular in autumn. When it splits, keep right and continue all the way to the apex of Polnoon Street and Montgomery Street where the woodland is left behind.

Turn left and descend Montgomery Street, soon passing The Carswell Centre. This is home to six sculptures by William Gemmell (1814–1891), a joiner by trade who lived all his life in Eaglesham. Between 1842 and 1845 the self-taught sculptor also created 15 life-size stone statues representing the family circle described in Robert Burns' poem 'The Cotter's Saturday Night'. Sadly, however, after being exhibited to great acclaim in London and purchased by an unknown party, they went missing and their whereabouts are still not known.

Beyond Mid Road the route reaches the 18th-century Eaglesham Parish Church. The name Eaglesham is derived from *Eaglais* – Gaelic for 'church' – and *ham*, an Anglo-Saxon word

for 'village'. Within the graveyard is the Covenanter's Memorial which commemorates the death of two local men, Robert Lockhart and Gabriel Thomson, who attended an illegal Coventicle on Eaglesham Moor on 5 May 1685. They were hunted down and shot on the open moorland by a party of Highland Dragoons for defending, according to the memorial, 'presbytery against prelacy'.

From the church descend back to Gilmour Street, turn left and return to the start.

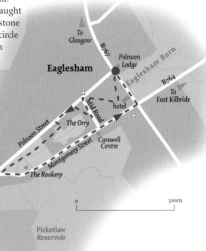

Eaglesham and the Dripps

Distance 9.5km **Time** 2 hours 30
Terrain quiet country roads; the ford may
be impassable when the river is in spate
Map OS Explorer 334 **Access** buses to
Eaglesham from Glasgow

**This walk is almost entirely on quiet
country roads around the conservation
village of Eaglesham.**

The route begins from the corner of
Gilmour Street and Polnoon Street in
Eaglesham village centre. It was built as
a planned village in 1769 and developed
around its agriculture and a number of
grain and cottonmills. It may surprise
many that Eaglesham was threatened
with demolition in the 1940s. However,
a group of local residents recognised the
value of its rich architectural heritage and
campaigned for it to be saved.

Facing Polnoon Lodge, turn left to
follow Gilmour Street for 250m, then turn

right onto Holehouse Road. Descend
past Eaglesham Cemetery, at which point
the pavement ends. The route now
proceeds as a narrow road away from
Eaglesham (keep an eye out for traffic),
later passing beneath the A726. An old
ford then crosses the White Cart – when
the river is in spate the road will be
closed at this point.

Once across, the road climbs gently
alongside hedgerows through a bucolic
landscape, with fine views across the
surrounding farmland. Where the road
splits, keep right for Thorntonhall all the
way to Peel Road. Turn left and follow the
roadside verge, passing several impressive
stone villas, including South Hill of Dripps.

There are a few Dripps on this walk.
Land in the area was once granted to a
Norman baron called Le Drep and over
time it became Le Drip. Farmers often
took their surname from their land and

o Dripps became a common
ocal moniker.

When you meet Waterfoot
Road, turn left and follow this,
njoying views across Glasgow
o the Campsie Fells and even Ben
omond on a clear day. Beyond
North Hill of Dripps, the road
veaves its way onwards, soon
assing Townhead of Dripps and
hen Meikle Dripps. As the road
weeps left, the views extend
cross Busby and Clarkston
vith the road flanked by ash,
irch and beech woodland.

After nearly 2km, leave
Vaterfoot Road by turning left
nto another narrow road,
signposted for Eaglesham. The
oad rises gradually before levelling off
o pass a farmhouse with a lovely outlook
ver Waterfoot. Look out for traffic on a
couple of tight bends as you continue,
with the road soon rising gently to pass
hrough a little pocket of trees. It is worth
stopping here to look back at the view
hat stretches across East Renfrewshire all
he way to the Southern Highlands.

At a fork, carry straight on, enjoying the
view out to Eaglesham Moor. This was
where Rudolf Hess, Adolf Hitler's deputy
and named successor, parachuted from a
small Messerschmitt fighter before it
crashed after flying solo nearly 1600km
from Munich in May 1941. He was met by
a local farmer with a pitchfork who

marched him to the local Home Guard.
It is thought that Hess hoped to end the
war before Germany invaded Russia and
that he flew to Scotland without the
approval of his Führer because he believed
the Duke of Hamilton could persuade the
British leadership to surrender. Hess was
found guilty of war crimes at the
Nuremberg Trials and sentenced to life
imprisonment. He committed suicide in
Spandau Prison in 1987 at the age of 93.

Carry on all the way back to the outward
route south of Thortonhall. Turn right
and retrace your steps, surrounded by
wonderful scenic countryside, to return
to Eaglesham.

◀ Straw bales near Eaglesham

Rouken Glen

Distance 4.5km **Time** 1 hour 30
Terrain parkland paths and tracks
Map OS Explorer 342 **Access** trains to
Whitecraigs from Glasgow and Neilston;
buses to Rouken Glen from Glasgow

In a city renowned for its parkland,
Rouken Glen Park is one of Glasgow's
finest. Named after Rokandmyll, a mill
that used to lie within the estate
grounds, its history dates back to 1530
when James V gifted the lands to the 1st
Earl of Montgomery. This route follows
riverbank and glen paths to cascading
waterfalls and beautiful open parkland.
Fans of the big screen will also be
delighted to know that an infamous
scene involving an air-rifle and a
skinhead's dog from the cult 1990s' film
Trainspotting was shot here.

Whitecraigs Railway Station sits just
outside the park boundary and is a great
place to start the walk. Leaving the station,
turn left onto Davieland Road, then go
through a gate into Rouken Glen Park.
A path crosses the parkland to a fork.

Keep left down to a boating pond,
home to swans, coot, moorhen and
black-headed gulls. Winter visitors
include tufted duck and little grebe.
Bear left here and walk clockwise a short
distance to the pond's northwestern edge.
Go left onto another path and continue
past a waterfall before following a track
northwest through more parkland and
on into attractive woodland.

The track skirts the outer edge of the
woodland beside a golf course, soon
reaching a junction. Keep right and
continue, enjoying fine views across
Glasgow to the Kilpatrick Hills, Dumgoyne
and a distant Ben Lomond. A gradual
descent proceeds through beech trees all
the way to a leisure centre car park. Keep
left and follow the road through the car
park to Stewarton Road.

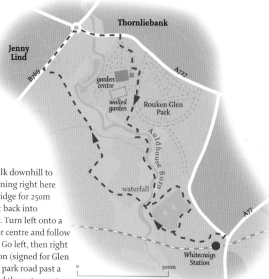

Thornliebank

Jenny Lind

B769

A727

garden centre

walled garden

Rouken Glen Park

Auldhouse Burn

waterfall

A77

Whitecraigs Station

0   500m

◀ Rouken Glen Park

Go right and walk downhill to a roundabout, turning right here to follow Spiersbridge for 250m before going right back into Rouken Glen Park. Turn left onto a path for the visitor centre and follow this to a junction. Go left, then right at the next junction (signed for Glen Walks) to follow a park road past a wildlife garden and the entrance to the Walled Garden, which dates from the late 19th century. Originally designed as a kitchen garden, it was converted into an ornamental garden when the estate was gifted to Glasgow in 1906.

Bear right onto a path (again for Glen Walks) and continue to a junction. Go left into woodland and drop down steps to reach more steps on the right. Descend these over a footbridge spanning the fast-flowing Auldhouse Burn (look out for dipper and kingfisher), then keep left. Now head upstream through a delightful wooded gorge. The path rises gently to a flight of steps on the left, which descend to another bridge spanning the river.

Once across, turn right up a steep flight of steps, after which the wooded path continues high above the river, soon reaching a spectacular waterfall viewpoint – several tiers cascade down into the gorge below. Once across a footbridge, turn left and follow a paved path through a line of beech trees with distant views of the Campsie Fells.

Take the first path on the right and climb back to the boating pond. Carry straight on around the pond, passing a café, and return to the outward path. Go left to retrace your steps to Davieland Road and Whitecraigs Railway Station.

Fereneze Braes and Killoch Glen

Distance 7.5km **Time** 2 hours 30
Terrain golf course, countryside paths
and tracks, pavement, minor road
Map OS Explorer 342 **Access** trains to
Barrhead from Glasgow; buses to
Barrhead from Paisley

**Rising above the town of Barrhead, the
Fereneze Braes offer some great walking
with a wilder air. At more than 200m
above sea level, Duchielaw is the highest
point of a walk that also takes in the
delights of Killoch Glen.**

From Barrhead Railway Station, follow
Paisley Road to Fereneze Avenue and turn
left. At its end, follow the access drive of
Fereneze Golf Club as it climbs to its

clubhouse. At the top right-hand corner
of the car park turn left onto a path which
rises steeply, sweeping right, then left to
emerge at the 18th green. Keeping an eye
out for golfers, the path continues west
on a steady climb along the right edge of
the fairway. Higher up, it is worth taking
a breather as the views across Barrhead
to Glasgow are excellent.

At a junction turn left, carefully follow
a track across the fairway to its left edge
and turn right. A gradual ascent along the
edge of the fairway continues, with more
views of the Campsie Fells, Kilpatrick Hills
and Neilston Pad. Aim for two radio
masts that soon come into view, all the
way to a fence. Here turn right to follow

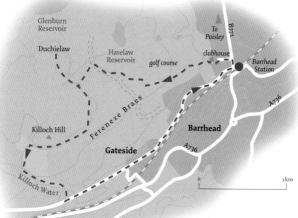

a grassy track past the 15th, then 14th, tees. Drop down to a junction, where you keep left for Killoch Glen, following a track for a few metres. Now bear left at a marker post from where a path rises gradually above the golf course and Harelaw Dam.

Bear left when the path splits to reach a gate and, once through, go right onto a farm track, enjoying views across Glasgow. Keep on for 200m, then turn left through a gate, again signed for Killoch Glen. A grassy path runs between a wall and fence through another gate. Keep straight Paisley and Glenburn.

Beyond a gate follow a boggy path over a footbridge and up onto Duchielaw, its summit marked with a small cairn. The view takes in the Luss Hills, Ben Lomond and the Arrochar Alps. Retrace your steps back to the sign, then turn right through a gate for Killoch Glen.

A mixture of grassy path and boardwalk crosses the hillside and passes through two gates. Roe deer, skylark and kestrel may be seen; there are also views of Neilston. After descending a steep flight of wooden steps towards Killoch Glen, pass through two more gates with the path then swinging left to a signpost. Turn right here and go down more steps into beautiful mixed woodland for a lovely descent through Killoch Glen, alongside the Killoch Water and a series of waterfalls. Keep right at the next two forks all the way to Gateside Road.

Turn left and follow this very pleasant stretch of quiet road into the small settlement of Gateside. A final 1.75km walk leads back to the station.

◄ Glasgow from Fereneze Braes

17

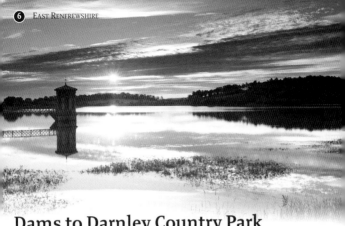

Dams to Darnley Country Park

**Distance 11.25km Time 3 hours 30
Terrain paths and tracks, minor road
Map OS Explorer 342 Access no public
transport to the start**

Dams to Darnley Country Park sits above
the town of Barrhead and straddles the
border of East Renfrewshire and
Glasgow. It also has one of the best views
of Glasgow. This out-and-back walk takes
in the dams of Balgray, Ryat Linn and
Waulkmill, which were constructed
during the 1840s when industrial
Glasgow struggled to supply enough
clean drinking water for its ever growing
population. The dams no longer supply
water to Glasgow but, along with the
surrounding terrain, provide an area for
wildlife to thrive.

The route begins from Balgraystone car
park, which is situated 500m south of
Springfield Road in Barrhead. From the
south end of the car park, turn briefly left

onto a path signposted for Waulkmill
Glen and then fork right to skirt anti-
clockwise around Balgray Reservoir, home
to the largest population of breeding
great crested grebes within Renfrewshire,
East Renfrewshire and Inverclyde.
Migrants such as Icelandic black-tailed
godwits, whooper swans and barnacle
geese also use the reservoir to rest and
refuel before continuing their long
journeys north or south. Tufted ducks,
ringed plover, redshank and common
sandpiper may well be spied at different
times of the year.

The path hugs the line of the reservoir,
with far-reaching views of Glasgow,
Dumgoyne, the Campsie Fells and the
Southern Highlands, including Ben
Lomond. After 2km, the path reaches the
busy Aurs Road. The structure to the left
is a draw-off or intake tower and is a
Grade B-listed building.

Carefully cross Aurs Road onto an access

Waulkmill Reservoir

road (watch out for park traffic) which descends to the left of the Brock Burn before it sweeps right to pass the dramatic Ryat Linn (*Linn* is the Scots word for 'waterfall'). The road now heads northeast alongside Ryat Linn Reservoir all the way to a fork. Keep left to drop down beneath a red-brick railway viaduct and walk downhill between Littleton and Waulkmill Glen Reservoirs. The road veers left before splitting again, dropping down from here into the woodland of Waulkmill Glen, an important ancient semi-natural woodland and a Site of Special Scientific Interest due to the carboniferous limestone within the glen.

In a while the road (now for all traffic) passes through peaceful countryside, later crossing a bridge over the Brock Burn as it approaches Darnley. Almost immediately, turn right from the road and follow a firm path through woodland. At a junction go right and follow another path to where it splits. Bear left, then right back onto the road and follow it all the way to Nitshill Road (A726). Carefully cross the A726 at traffic lights to reach the venerable Darnley Sycamore.

It is said that it was under this tree in 1567 that Mary, Queen of Scots collected her smallpox-ridden second husband (and first cousin) Henry Stewart, Lord Darnley, and returned with him to Edinburgh as he was too weak to ride a horse on his own. Darnley was killed a few days later when his Edinburgh residence, the Kirk o' Field, was blown up on the instructions of the Earl of Bothwell, who soon after this became Mary's third husband.

Retrace your steps through Waulkmill Glen to Aurs Road to return to the start.

Balgray and Ryat Linn Reservoirs

Distance 5.25km Time 1 hour 30
Terrain country park access roads and
paths, field edges Map OS Explorer 342
Access no public transport to the start

Dams to Darnley Country Park,
which sits above the town of Barrhead,
includes a number of habitats, such as
woodland, grassland and scrub. It covers
1350 acres and is a Site of Special
Scientific Interest due to the geology to
be found within it. However, it is the
dams, which sit at its heart, that are the
park's most popular feature. This lovely
route visits four of the dams with a string
of views and loads of wildlife to enjoy
along the way.

The route begins from Balgraystone car
park, which is situated 500m south of
Springfield Road in Barrhead. Take the
path at the northeastern edge of the car
park and follow this northeast near to
Balgray Reservoir. The path soon rises
gently, running to the right of a metal
fence and a railway line, with some fine
views along the reservoir. When
the path sweeps left to cross a railway
bridge, leave it by bearing right onto a
grassy path. This continues to the right
of the fence and descends all the way
to Aurs Road.

This is a busy road so take care
crossing it, then go through a gate into
a field. Follow its left edge as it rises
gradually east, still to the right of the
railway line. At the top of the climb, a firm
track is picked up which drops downhill,
soon curving left to a bridge, where it

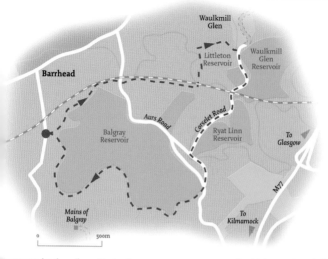

passes under the railway. The track continues north between fields for 250m, swinging right and then left to reach a small stand of trees.

Turn right from the track and follow the edge of a field to the right of a hedge, where the view extends across Glasgow to the Campsie Fells. This leads all the way down to woodland where you turn right to continue along the field edge to a gate. Once through, cross a bridge over the Brock Burn to reach the Dams to Darnley Country Park access road. Keeping an eye out for park traffic, turn right and follow the road between Waulkmill and Littleton Reservoirs. Depending on the season, within the hedgerows and out on the water, sedge and willow warbler, redwing, fieldfare, wigeon, teal, goldeneye, lapwing, ringed plover and goosander,

amongst many other birds, may be spied.

The road curves right to rise gradually and pass beneath a red-brick railway viaduct. Beyond this, keep right at a fork and continue along the banks of Ryat Linn Reservoir, a good place to spot dragonflies and damselflies during the summer months. The road, flanked with oak and beech trees, soon reaches a junction beside the Ryat Linn.

Go left and continue on a gradual climb back to Aurs Road. Again, carefully cross the road onto a path that hugs the shores of Balgray Reservoir. It is a straightforward 2km back to the car park with no navigational issues, allowing you to enjoy the expansive scenery and varied wildlife; Fereneze Braes, Glasgow, the Campsie Fells and Ben Lomond are all visible on a clear day.

Duncarnock

Distance 5.5km **Time** 1 hour 30
Terrain minor roads, field and hillside
paths **Map** OS Explorer 342
Access no public transport to the start

With its rounded profile rising to 204m
above sea level, Duncarnock is always
present when exploring the landscape
surrounding Barrhead and Neilston.
Known locally as The Craigie,
Duncarnock's summit holds the remains
of a fort that may date back some 3000
years. Parking is limited nearby, so it is
best to begin from **Balgraystone car park**
and take the quiet scenic roads to the
base of Duncarnock.

Balgraystone car park is situated 500m
south of Springfield Road in Barrhead.

Turn left out of the car park and, keeping
an eye out for traffic, follow Balgraystone
Road as it winds south away from Balgra
Reservoir. Beyond the remains of a stone
cottage the road rises gradually up to
Glanderston Road.

Turn right and follow this narrow
road through a scenic portion of East
Renfrewshire, with the outline of
Duncarnock soon coming into view. After
a short descent and ascent, Glanderston
Road curves sharply to the right. Leave it
here by turning left onto an access road
for Glanderston Mains. Follow this for
150m, then turn right through a gate.

After a few metres, cross a stile on the
left and follow a grass embankment abov
Glanderston Dam, always popular with

anglers, as well as moorhen, tufted duck and goldeneye. Cross a low fence beside four plane trees. This was once the site of Glanderston House, which was built at the end of the 17th century around the ruin of an old towerhouse. Edward Arthur Walton, one of the 'Glasgow Boys' group of artists who became prominent in the 1880s and '90s, was born here in 1860.

Glanderston Dam used to supply water to local printworks and bleachfields. On 30 December 1842 the dam burst its banks during a wild storm and eight people from the same family, who lived near the printworks below the dam, lost their lives.

At the end of the embankment, turn left, go over a stile and a footbridge at the outflow of the dam and then turn right. Cross a field, to the left of a row of trees, then bear right. Continue across the field, then go over a stile in a wall. Keep left and follow an uneven path beneath the steep northeastern slopes of Duncarnock. The path curves right and begins to climb sharply to a fork. Keep right and continue west, ascending steep slopes, crossing the low wall that marks the

ramparts of the old fort, to reach the top.

It is thought that the fort was occupied around 1500 to 3000 years ago. Its position would have given those living here a prime vantage point. The panorama extends across Balgray Reservoir and Glasgow to the Campsie Fells, with the volcanic plug of Dumgoyne a prominent landmark. Mountains such as Ben Lomond and Ben Ledi can be seen beyond. A good portion of East Renfrewshire's rolling countryside spreads east and south from Duncarnock.

From the top, carefully retrace your steps to Glanderston Dam, then follow the road back to the start.

◀ View from Duncarnock Fort

Neilston Pad

Distance 6.5km Time 2 hours
Terrain countryside paths and tracks,
pavement Map OS Explorer 342
Access trains to Neilston from Glasgow;
buses to Neilston from Paisley

At 261m above sea level, Neilston Pad
is one of the highest points in East
Renfrewshire and is a great place for
far-reaching views. This circular route
traverses the slopes of Neilston Pad, as
well as exploring the countryside
surrounding Neilston. Some of the paths
can be muddy.

The walk begins from Neilston Railway
Station. From here, turn right and follow
Kingston Road through Neilston. After
750m turn left onto a stony track and

follow this as it winds its way southeast
through picturesque countryside where
buzzard and kestrel may well be seen.

In a while, the track curves sharp right
to pass Craig o' Neilston Farm, after which
it rises gradually through a gate. Continue
on a gentle ascent with the rounded
slopes of Neilston Pad ahead. Looking
back, fine views across Glasgow begin to
open out. When the track splits, keep left
and follow it across a field where cattle
may be grazing. Carry on as it sweeps
right and descends gently through a gate.
Leave the track behind here and bear right
onto a muddy and initially ill-defined
path that rises gradually into woodland,
skirting the left edge and lower wooded
slopes of Neilston Pad.

◄ Tinto Hill from Neilston Pad

The path levels off and improves underfoot as you enjoy views extending across Snypes Dam to Duncarnock Fort.

Soon, the path begins to climb steadily to the left of a fence and a wall to reach a fork. Keep right and climb a short distance to a gate where the peaks of Arran and Tinto Hill may be visible on a clear day. Go through the gate and climb the path north, to the right of the fence, onto the broad, flat summit which is marked with a small cairn. A magnificent outlook extends southwest across Renfrewshire and Ayrshire and north over Glasgow to the Campsie Fells, the Southern Highlands and Ben Lomond.

Return to the gate. Once through keep straight on and descend a grassy path south, passing through another gate. Soon you can see Harelaw Dam. The path winds downhill, eventually dropping to a short muddy section. The path bears left here, then right through a small pocket of conifer trees to reach a track.

Turn right, then right again and follow another track, soon sweeping right past a number of beech trees before descending to Craighall Dam, a fine spot for a break where swans, coot and moorhen can be seen out on the water. The track, flanked by woodland, now heads northeast for 600m to a gate before leading through

open countryside with fine views of Neilston Pad and East Renfrewshire.

Beyond two more gates descend to the outward route, bearing left here to retrace your steps past Craig o' Neilston Farm to Kingston Road. Turn right and return to the start.

Cowden Hall and Midgehole Glen

Distance 6.75km Time 2 hours 30
Terrain countryside paths and tracks,
pavement Map OS Explorer 342
Access trains to Neilston from Glasgow;
buses to Neilston from Paisley

The village of Neilston is surrounded
by countryside with lots of paths and
tracks to discover and explore. This walk
visits the estate of Cowden Hall and the
peaceful surrounds of Midgehole Glen,
also known as Midge Glen.

Begin from Neilston Railway Station.
Turn left to follow Station Road to Main
Street. Keep left and walk through
Neilston for 250m, then turn right onto
Holehouse Brae, which descends steeply
with views of the Lochliboside Hills to
reach Crofthead Mill. This was built in
1880 to replace the original cottonmill
which was destroyed by fire in 1792.
Powered by the Levern Water, Crofthead
was one of several mills that made
Neilston an important centre for the
textile industry from the late 19th
century, and it is now a listed building.

Turn left and follow Crofthead Road
past Crofthead Cottages to join a path at
the road end. Immediately turn right to
follow a track that leads through Cowden
Hall Estate, established by millowner
James Orr in 1830 on the site of the 'auld
castle' of Cowden. His son, Robert Orr,
later built the magnificent but sadly long
gone Cowden Hall and further developed
the grounds. After being used during the
First World War to house Belgian and
British soldiers, the tennis courts,
bowling greens, orchards and billiard
room were opened up for local
millworkers to enjoy.

At a junction take the centre of three
paths, which sweeps left and descends
into a secluded glen where chaffinch,

greenfinch and goldcrest may be spotted. Upon reaching a fence the path veers left along the edge of woodland, soon gaining a fork. Keep right, exit the woodland, bear left and follow a path, then track along the left edge of a field to a bridge spanning the Levern Water.

Once across, a path rises to a rough road. Turn right and walk to Uplawmoor Road, turning right here. Follow a pavement, then roadside verge, again crossing the Levern Water. After another 70m bear left through a gate onto a track which heads southwest through attractive countryside. After passing under an old railway bridge, a steady climb brings you to a fork. Keep left to follow a path rising through the wooded confines of Midgehole Glen, high above the river and a waterfall. Local tradition has it that the name Midgehole Glen is a corruption of 'Imagehole Glen', so named after an image of the Virgin Mary was dashed on the rocks here during the Reformation.

At a minor road, turn left and follow it as it climbs steeply, then levels off with views towards the Campsies. At Kingston Road, turn left for 100m before going right through a gate, where a path splits. Take the right branch and walk towards Neilston Quarry, which is popular with climbers.

At the quarry base go right, then right again at a fork and ascend a path to a crossroads. Turning right, descend to a track – ahead is the rounded profile of Neilston Pad. Turn left to go through a gate and drop downhill through two more gates to a junction where there is a stunning view of Glasgow. Beyond another gate, pass Craig o' Neilston Farm. From here, the track continues all the way to Kingston Road. Turn right and follow the pavement for 750m back to the start.

Heading into Renfrewshire the landscape is principally urban and its history industrial. The town of Paisley is the region's focal point and its largest, with an array of imperial buildings and a fascinating textile manufacturing heritage. It is also home to a magnificent abbey, which dates from the 12th century and where, it is thought, the patriot William Wallace was educated by the learned monks.

Against this industrial backdrop are unexpected pockets of beauty, including Jenny's Well Nature Reserve and Gleniffer Braes Country Park, which rises just to the south of Paisley, its wildlife-rich moorland and wooded countryside sitting in stark contrast to the brick and sandstone of the town's architecture.

Nearby, situated on the banks of both the River Clyde and the White Cart Water, the historic port of Renfrew is the former county town of Renfrewshire. A fine walk takes in stretches of both rivers. The majestic River Clyde also forms the basis of a scenic walk around Mar Hall Estate, where the outlook extends along the river to the rolling Kilpatrick Hills and the birdlife includes oystercatcher, shag and redshank.

Paisley and Renfrew

Gleniffer Braes

Distance 4km Time 1 hour 30
Terrain tracks and paths
Map OS Explorer 342 Access no public
transport to the start

**Gleniffer Braes Country Park rises to the
south of Paisley. The park is 5km long
and 1.5km wide and covers an area of 1300
acres, with a variety of walking trails to
follow, on the edge of Renfrewshire's
urban sprawl.**

The walk begins from Robertson car
park, known locally as the 'car park in
the sky' due to the wonderful views
extending across Paisley and Glasgow to
the Southern Highlands. It sits just under
5km southwest of Paisley town centre.
Take the grassy track that rises south past
a children's play area to a gate. Once
through, carry straight on, following an
indistinct grassy track southeast across
Gleniffer Braes.

This grassland and surrounding
woodland is home to a range of birdlife,
such as buzzard, kestrel, wheatear,
sparrowhawk, meadow pipit and skylark,
while Highland cattle also graze the land.
At certain times of the year, orchids, wild
pansies, harebell and waxcap fungi can be
found here.

The track soon sweeps left and, after a
large solitary tree, a solid track continues
southeast. Beyond a gate, cross Sergeant
Law Road into Sergeant Law car park. Take
the centre of three gates and keep to the
right edge of the braes, following a grassy
path to the left of a fence and Paisley Golf
Course, with views to Dumgoyne and the
Campsie Fells. After crossing a small
footbridge, the track descends gradually
northeast, with a spectacular view of
Glasgow ahead. Soon it passes a wooden
post, marked with horseshoes, near
Paisley Golf Course clubhouse.

Gleniffer Braes

Bear left to follow a vague path heading in a westerly direction along the lip of the Braes. There are a few wooden posts to aid navigation if visibility is poor. However, on a clear day the scenery is magnificent with Ben Lomond and Ben More, some 30km to the north, rising beyond Paisley and the Kilpatrick Hills. When the path splits keep left and continue on a gradual uphill climb. This leads to a more obvious path where a left turn takes you upstream along the east bank of the Gleniffer Burn, all the way to a bridge on the right.

Once across keep right and follow the fast-flowing burn downstream along a grassy path heading northwest towards a pocket of woodland – keep an eye out for roe deer. Upon gaining a paved path turn

left and follow this through woodland all the way back to Sergeant Law Road. Beyond a gate, cross the road, then pass through another gate.

Keep right onto the Tannahill Walkway, named after Robert Tannahill, who was born in Paisley in 1774 and became well known during his short life as the 'Weaver Poet' in the wake of the 'Ploughman Poet' Robert Burns. He is perhaps best remembered for the words which became the basis for the song 'Wild Mountain Thyme', with the chorus of 'Will Ye Go, Lassie, Go'.

The path again skirts the edge of the Braes with more fine views of Paisley. Beyond a gate, turn left onto a path which rises gently all the way back to the start.

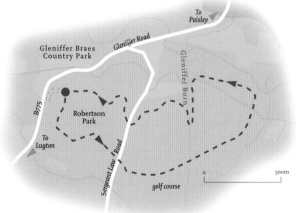

Brownside Braes and Glen Park

Distance 4km Time 1 hour 30
Terrain tracks and paths
Map OS Explorer 342 Access buses to
Brownside Farm road end from Paisley
and Barrhead

Brownside Braes, an extension of Gleniffer Braes, sit at the eastern edge of Gleniffer Braes Country Park. Paths and tracks run along the base of the Braes and then through the woodland surrounding Glen Park Dams. Fine scenery, lots of wildlife and interesting sites associated with Robert Tannahill all add to the joy of this route.

Brownside Farm car park is situated a short distance off Caplethill Road, which is 1.5km and 3.5km from Barrhead and Paisley town centres respectively. Turn right from the car park and follow an access track through a gate, passing Brownside Farmhouse. The track then

curves right through another gate, signed for Glen Park. A gradual rise now continues west along a wooded track before it travels through open countryside at the base of Brownside Braes with stunning views across Paisley to Ben Lomond.

Soon afterwards, where the track splits, branch right and continue, enjoying views that stretch to the Arrochar Alps. The track can be muddy as it passes through a gate to cross a field. Much of the grassland here is grazed by Highland cattle. They are docile but dogs should be kept on leads. During the summer months, look out for wild pansy, northern marsh orchids and an array of butterflies. Redwing, kestrel, buzzard and even whitethroat are some of the birds that may be spotted here.

Carry on to reach another gate at the edge of woodland. Once through, bear left and follow a path in the trees to a

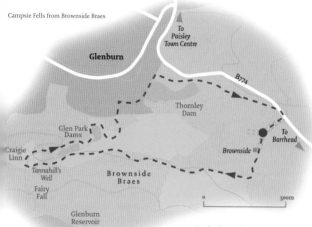

Campsie Fells from Brownside Braes

To Paisley Town Centre

Glenburn

B774

Thornley Dam

Glen Park Dams

To Barrhead

Craigie Linn

Brownside

Tannahill's Well

Brownside Braes

Fairy Fall

Glenburn Reservoir

0   500m

poems including 'The Braes o' Gleniffer'. Sadly, Tannahill suffered with mental health problems and in 1810 he took his own life, aged only 35.

Continue downstream to the right of the river, cross a footbridge, then go up steps. Turn right where a path heads downstream, passing the Upper and Lower Reservoirs. At the outflow of the Lower Reservoir, go right and follow a path along its edge, then turn left down steps. Turn right onto a track which rises to a junction where you go left. Drop downhill on an access road and exit Gleniffer Braes Country Park by turning right onto Glenfield Road. Follow the pavement for 300m past Thornley Dam, then go right onto a shared-use path signed for Barrhead. Follow this to its end, turn right and return to the car park.

unction just above the Lower Reservoir f Glen Park Dams. Turn left to a fork, ear right and follow this past the Upper eservoir. When the path splits again, eep left before climbing some steps. At junction go right, ascend gradually to a ork, go left up more steps, then turn right nto a path waymarked for a waterfall.

Once down a flight of steps, it is worth urning left to walk the short distance to each the waterfall. Return past the steps nd follow a burn downstream, passing he Tannahill Well and the Tannahill Birken Tree. This was planted in 1974 o mark the bi-centenary of Robert Tannahill's birth. Born in Paisley in 1774, Tannahill wrote more than 100 songs and

Jenny's Well

Distance 2.5km **Time** 1 hour
Terrain paths **Map** OS Explorer 342
Access buses to Jennys Well Road from
Paisley town centre

Surrounded by the urban sprawl of
Paisley, Jenny's Well Local Nature Reserve
is a haven for wildlife and a lovely
tranquil spot for a wander, especially
when you consider that it was once a
site for heavy industry. Having been
designated a Local Nature Reserve in 1996
chaffinch, kingfisher, heron and even
otter may well be spotted along the
network of paths and the banks of the
White Cart Water.

There is parking on Jennys Well Road
and ample parking on the adjacent
Hawkhead Road. At the end of Jennys
Well Road go around a barrier onto a
shared-use path and follow this west
along the wooded fringes of the nature

reserve. Soon the woodland is left behind
and the path crosses parkland with good
views of the Kilpatrick Hills; the rounded
lump of Duncolm, the highest point of
the Kilpatricks, is particularly prominent.

Exit the parkland onto Whinhill Road,
then take the second path on the right
into Jenny's Well Local Nature Reserve.
The landscape here was heavily quarried
during the 19th century for limestone and
whinstone and later it was home to
Jenny's Well Laundry, after which the site
was used for landfill and allotments.
Thankfully, after careful management,
nature has returned.

A path runs along the edge of the
wood parallel with Cathcart Crescent.
At a crossroads, carry straight on and
continue – with Abbey Mill and its
enormous red-brick chimney soon
coming into view – all the way to a
footbridge. Ignore this; instead stay on

the path as it curves round to reach the banks of the White Cart Water, just before the Blackhall Railway Viaduct.

This was originally built by Thomas Telford and John Rennie in the early 1800s as an aqueduct for the Glasgow, Paisley & Johnstone Canal. When the canal closed in 1881, it was widened and converted into a railway line. The bridge is thought to be the longest single-span masonry aqueduct of the canal age on a British canal and one of the world's first railway-carrying bridges. John Rennie went on to design the first Waterloo Bridge over the

River Thames which featured nine arches, each spanning nearly 40m.

Continue alongside the river before looping round to return to the outward route beside the footbridge. Bear left, retrace your steps to the crossroads and turn left again for another loop through the reserve, soon rising gently back to the outward path. Turn left, leave the reserve onto Whinhill Road, then go left again back into parkland.

Turn left to follow a path along the edge of the park, with fine views of the Campsie Fells. As the path swings right, bear left onto another path which drops down into more attractive woodland above the river. At a junction turn left to reach the next junction where you keep left to walk through a small clearing, ignoring a path on the right. On reaching a fork, go left down a flight of steps, cross a path, descend more steps, then make a final left turn and walk the short distance back to the start.

Blackhall

White Cart Water

Jenny's Well

To Paisley town centre

Todholm Road

A726

Jennys Well Road

0 250m

35

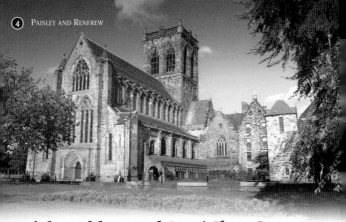

Paisley Abbey and Sma' Shot Cottages

Distance 2.5km Time 1 hour
Terrain pavement Map OS Explorer 342
Access trains from Inverclyde, Ayrshire
and Glasgow; buses from Glasgow

The town of Paisley developed
around its abbey, founded in the 12th
century, and grew as an important centre
of weaving during the Industrial
Revolution. This route visits the abbey
and the Sma' Shot Cottages, as well
as historic lanes and some other fine
civic buildings and statues.

The walk begins from County Square in
the town centre; during the 1800s this was
the site of the County Prison. Follow
Gilmour Street to Gauze Street beside the
Paisley Cenotaph. Turn left and pass the
impressive town hall, then go right onto
Abbey Close and pass the statues of Sir
Peter Coats, Sir Thomas Coats (of the
famous thread manufacturing Coats
family), ornithologist and poet Alexander

Wilson, Robert Tannahill, the 'Weaver
Poet', and the manufacturer George
Aitken Clark. Carry on to reach the
remarkable Paisley Abbey.

Building began in 1163 after Walter
Fitzalan, the High Steward of Scotland,
signed a charter for a monastery to be
built on his lands. Paisley Abbey became
an important commercial centre for trade
across Europe with great influence and
wealth following. It is thought that a
young William Wallace was educated
by the well-travelled monks here –
arguments still rage as to whether Wallace
was born nearby in Elderslie or in the
Ayrshire village of Ellerslie. Paisley Abbey
retains its medieval nave and its 19th-
century stained-glass windows.

Take a right onto Bridge Street, cross
Abbey Bridge that spans the White Cart
Water, then turn right onto the River Cart
Walk and follow the paved path alongside
the river, enjoying views of the abbey and

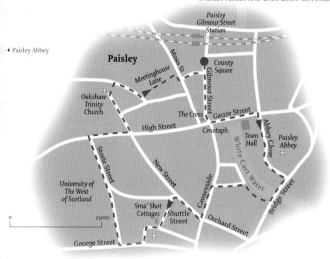

◄ Paisley Abbey

Paisley

Paisley Gilmour Street Station

County Square

Moss St

Gilmour Street

Meetinghouse Lane

Oakshaw Trinity Church

Gauze Street

The Cross

High Street

Abbey Close

Cenotaph

Town Hall

Paisley Abbey

Storie Street

White Cart Water

New Street

University of The West of Scotland

Causeyside

Bridge Street

Sma' Shot Cottages

Shuttle Street

Orchard Street

George Street

0   250m

the town hall. At Forbes Place, go left, then left again onto Causeyside Street before turning right onto New Street. The first left turn off New Street leads to Shuttle Street and the Sma' Shot Cottages. These historic buildings contain tangible evidence of Paisley's weaving heritage, including the Paisley design, or Paisley Pattern, that the town is renowned for. The teardrop motif, known as the *buta*, originated in Persia but came to Paisley via Indian adaptations, especially in the form of Kashmir shawls.

The cottages were built in the 1750s and contain the original weaving looms, giving an insight into what family life would have been like during the height of Paisley's manufacturing heyday.

Carry on to George Place, going right, then right again onto George Street

before turning right up Storie Street. This climbs gradually to the High Street. Turn right to reach Church Hill and then go left up this cobblestone lane. It climbs steeply all the way to the 18th-century High Kirk (now known as the Oakshaw Trinity Church), adorned by a magnificent steeple. This street has played an important role in the religious and educational history of Paisley; during the 19th century the street was home to the town's grammar school.

At the top, turn right onto Oakshaw Street East. Go right again and, after 100m, go left down the cobblestone Meetinghouse Lane with the wall on the right being all that remains of Paisley's Commercial School. At the end of the lane go right onto Moss Street, then left onto County Place to return to County Square.

Paisley mills and museums

Distance 4.25km Time 1 hour 30
Terrain pavement Map OS Explorer 342
Access trains to Paisley from Inverclyde,
Ayrshire and Glasgow; buses to Paisley
from Glasgow

Few places in Scotland, outwith the
major cities, can boast of such fine civic
architecture as Paisley. A wander around
the town passes a number of these
historic and important buildings.

Begin from County Square, a lively
pedestrianised area with several pubs and
cafés. Pass under the railway line of
Gilmour Street Station to reach Old
Sneddon Street and turn right. Follow the
pavement across Abercorn Bridge
spanning the White Cart Water and
continue along Weir Street before going
right onto Renfrew Road. This
then becomes Incle Street,
home of the striking St Mirin's Cathedral
and a statue of St Mirin, the patron saint
of Paisley. Also known as Mirren of
Benchor, he was prior of Bangor Abbey in
County Down before he crossed the Irish
Sea in the early 7th century to found a
religious community here. The town's
football team, St Mirren, take their name
from him and, according to local lore, play
in a black- and white-striped strip because
the Cluniac monks of Paisley Abbey wore
black and white robes.

Cross Incle Street onto Mill Street and
head south to Seedhill Road. Turn left and
walk 400m to a roundabout, then bear
right onto Benn Avenue to reach the
magnificent red-brick Mile End Mill, now
a business centre. The buildings
(including the 74m-high boilerhouse
chimney) played a crucial role in
Scotland's thread industry and employed
thousands of local people
until the mill's closure
in 1923. Inside is the Paisley
Thread Mill Museum.
Retrace your steps to

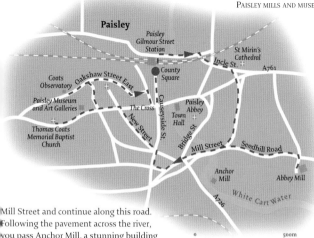

Mill Street and continue along this road. Following the pavement across the river, you pass Anchor Mill, a stunning building that was once home to a textile mill – it has since been converted into flats. Once over Bridge Street follow Gordon Street, then turn right onto Johnston Street. At its end go right onto Causeyside Street, then left onto New Street. Keep right when the road splits with a gradual ascent now taking you up to the High Street. Turn left and continue until you come to the Paisley Museum and Art Galleries.

When it opened in 1871, this was Scotland's first municipal museum. It was paid for by Sir Peter Coats (1808-1890) of the Coats weaving and thread manufacturing dynasty that became synonymous with Paisley. A huge employer, the Coats family bequeathed many buildings and public spaces to the people of Paisley, including the striking Thomas Coats Memorial Baptist Church, which stands a short distance west along the High Street.

Retrace your steps along the High Street as far as the steep Orr Square, where you turn left. At a junction turn right, then left to follow a cobbled lane climbing to Oakshaw Street East. A short distance to the left is the Coats Observatory, which first opened in 1883. It is the oldest public observatory in Scotland and contains a great collection of meteorological and seismological instruments. Walk back along Oakshaw Street East and descend to School Wynd. Bear left down to Moss Street and turn right to reach the High Street at the Paisley Cenotaph.

Ahead is the handsome town hall, which opened in 1882 and was named after George Clark, a member of the famous Clark thread family, who had left £20,000 in his will for its construction. A left turn along Gilmour Street leads back to County Square.

◀ Anchor Mill

The White Cart and the Clyde

Distance 6km **Time** 2 hours
Terrain pavement, parkland and riverside
paths **Map** OS Explorer 342 **Access** buses
to Renfrew from Glasgow and Paisley

The historic county town of Renfrew
sits a few miles north of Paisley and is
known as the 'Cradle of the Stewarts',
due to its early ties to the illustrious
royal house. The name Renfrew
translates from Cumbric as 'point of the
current' and is bounded by the Rivers
Cart and Clyde. This route follows the
banks of both rivers and visits the
peaceful surrounds of Robertson Park.

Start the walk beside the war memorial
at the corner of Hairst Street and
Inchinnan Road in Renfrew town centre.
Follow the pavement northeastwards past
the French gothic-style town hall. Carry
straight on along Canal Street, keeping
left on this as it becomes Ferry Road.
Continue along Ferry Road, over the

crossroads with Meadowside Street, to
reach the River Clyde and the slipway for
the historic Renfrew and Yoker Ferry. This
has operated for more than 200 years and
still transports thousands of passengers
across the river every year.

Return to Meadowside Street and turn
right to follow it for 300m before going
left onto a side road for the 'Clyde Coastal
Path'. After 50m go right, around a barrier,
onto a path for 'Inchinnan Road via the
River Clyde'. Follow this northwest, soon
picking up the River Clyde with fine views
to the Kilpatrick Hills. Beyond a green
navigation beacon – known locally as Wee
Blinky – the path reaches the confluence
of the Clyde and the River Cart, which is
followed upstream. It soon splits into the
Black and White Cart with the path
running south alongside the White Cart,
bearing right at a fork to pass the ancient
St Conval and Argyll Stones and reach
Inchinnan Road.

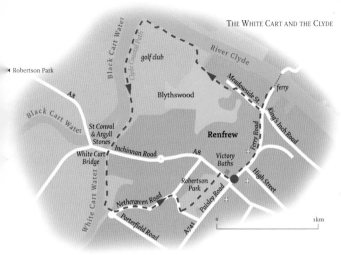

The fanciful story goes that, in the 6th century, St Conval floated on the stone across the Irish Sea to Scotland where he founded a church near Renfrew. The Argyll Stone marks where Archibald Campbell, 9th Earl of Argyll and enthusiastic Protestant, was captured while on the run, following his botched uprising against the Catholic King James VII. Together with his remaining loyal Campbell clansmen, he was captured after crossing the Clyde, tried for treason in Edinburgh and beheaded in 1685.

Cross Inchinnan Road beside the unusual bridge, the only functioning bascule bridge in Scotland; *bascule* is the French word for 'seesaw' and 'balance'. It was designed and built by Sir William Arrol & Co, the company that was also responsible for the construction of the Forth Bridge and Tower Bridge in London. Follow a footpath, signed Porterfield

Road, along the White Cart and continue on it as it curves left away from the river to reach a fork. Keep right here and upon reaching Porterfield Road turn left onto Nethergreen Road. Walk to Craigielea Road, taking the second exit at a roundabout. Continue to an entrance to Robertson Park.

Turn left and walk along a lovely beech-lined path. The park opened in 1912 and was gifted to the town by William Robertson, a local shipowner who started out as an office boy in Paisley. At Inchinnan Road exit right from the park and walk back to the start, passing the Edwardian Victory Baths, which opened in 1921 after they were gifted to the town by Lord and Lady Lobnitz, owners of a local shipbuilding company which built dredgers, floating docks, fishing boats and tugs, as well as more than 60 minor vessels for the Royal Navy.

The Clyde and Mar Hall Estate

Distance 6km Time 2 hours
Terrain pavement, woodland and
riverside paths Map OS Explorer 342
Access buses from Paisley and Clydebank
to Erskine Bridge, 750m from the start

A good network of paths runs along
the northern edge of Mar Hall Estate
and beside the mighty River Clyde as it
flows past Erskine towards Dumbarton.

There is ample parking at Boden Boo
car park, which sits just off the A726 a
little north of Erskine. It is thought that
the unusual name may refer to something
that is bow-shaped, possibly a local hill
or island; a nearby island named Bodin
Bow and later Botton Bow was indicated
on old maps.

Follow the Clyde Coastal Path west
through parkland, soon veering right to
pass under the Erskine Bridge which,
when opened in 1971, replaced the
Erskine to Old Kilpatrick ferry service

that had operated since 1777. Continue
alongside the River Clyde with views
extending to the Kilpatrick Hills, Bowling
and Lang Craigs. The river is tidal here so
sandy beaches may appear at lower tides
with oystercatcher, shag, redshank, curlew
and lapwing enjoying the spoils left by
the receding water.

Continue northwest, to the right of
Mar Hall Golf Course, with the impressive
Mar Hall dominating the grounds. Mar
was one of the seven Pictish kingdoms of
ancient Scotland and the Earl of Mar is the
oldest peerage in Britain, and possibly in
Europe. Mar Hall – originally known as
Erskine Mansion – was built between
1828 and 1845 before falling into disrepair
in the 20th century. After major
restoration it is now a hotel.

Further along the path the outline of
Dumbarton Rock appears, after which the
route peels left away from the River Clyde
and rises gently south between Mar Hall

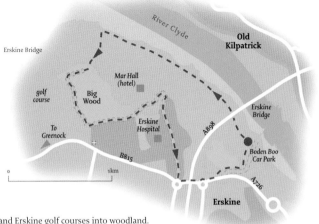

and Erskine golf courses into woodland. Almost immediately the path splits. Keep right to follow an initially muddy path through impressive woodland to a bench where a gap in the trees frames a view along the Clyde to Greenock. At a fork go right and continue along the edge of the wood to a small car park. Turn left and follow the Mar Hall access road all the way to a junction beside Mar Hall.

Once here turn left, then right through a small car park and right again. Climb a flight of steps onto Nursery Avenue and walk through the grounds of Erskine Hospital which, since 1916 when it opened as The Princess Louise Scottish Hospital for Limbless Sailors and Soldiers, has provided care and respite for British Armed Forces veterans who have settled in Scotland. It is now the largest ex-services facility in the country.

The road leads past the Reid Macewen Activity Centre, formerly a stable building dating from 1896, and a hexagonal piggery, both remnants of the old Mar Estate and now part of Erskine. Sir William Macewen was the chief surgeon at the hospital after the First World War who enlisted the help of engineers and craftsmen at local Yarrow Shipbuilders to design and manufacture the thousands of artificial limbs needed by returning servicemen.

Upon reaching the A726, turn left, follow the pavement under the Erskine Bridge and keep left at a roundabout. Where the pavement ends, turn left back onto the Clyde Coastal Path. At a fork keep right and descend, turning left onto another path just before it reaches a road. Carry on along this path and when it splits again go right; from here, it curves left. At a fork, take the right branch and return to the Boden Boo car park.

43

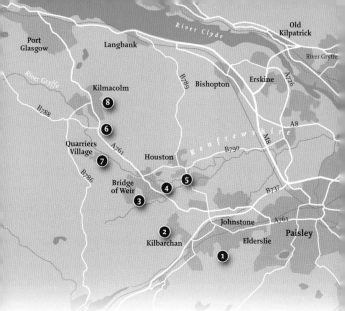

As you head west from Paisley, open countryside begins to dominate the landscape, especially around the many small towns and villages that punctuate the region. Right on the edge of the countryside is Johnstone, a town that has an industrial past but also two of the finest pockets of woodland in the local area – the bluebells during May and June are the star attraction.

The industrial backdrop is left behind by the time you reach Bridge of Weir. Yet there is still tangible evidence of the weaving and cotton industries that developed around the River Gryffe which cuts the town in two. Much can be learned about the textile industry that made Renfrewshire famous when visiting Kilbarchan and the Weaver's Cottage. Paths, tracks and minor roads make it easy to explore the scenery around both Bridge of Weir and Kilbarchan. Similarly, a walk from Houston to the Craigends Yew highlights the underrated beauty of the Renfrewshire landscape.

Almost imperceptibly, the border is crossed from Renfrewshire into Inverclyde where the villages of Quarriers and Kilmacolm give plenty of walking opportunities. The paths above Knapps Loch, near both settlements, offer views as far-reaching as Ben Lomond, while Glen Moss Wildlife Reserve in Kilmacolm is home, as you would expect, to a rich diversity of wildlife.

ohnstone to Kilmacolm

Johnstone and the Bluebell Woods

Distance 5km **Time** 1 hour 30
Terrain pavement, woodland paths
Map OS Explorer 342 **Access** trains to
Johnstone from Glasgow, Ayr, Ardrossan
and Largs; buses from Glasgow

The town of Johnstone, near Paisley, is
bounded to the south by two pockets of
woodland, known as Rannoch Wood and
Bluebell Wood – as the name suggests
the carpets of bluebells in late May are
spectacular. A mixture of pavement and
paths links both on a walk that also pays
a visit to Johnstone Castle. Johnstone is a
bustling little town that, like many of the
settlements within Renfrewshire,
developed during the Industrial
Revolution through the thread and
cotton industries.

Start from Johnstone Railway Station
where a right turn onto Thorn Brae leads
uphill to Overton Road. Turn right here

and follow the pavement past a number
of fine stone villas. At Beith Road bear
right and continue to reach Tower Road
on the left, signed for Johnstone Castle.
Walk uphill along this to reach the
16th-century towerhouse, surrounded
incongruously by modern housing.

The great Polish composer and
virtuoso pianist Frederic Chopin stayed at
Johnstone Castle in September 1848 as
part of a tour organised by his devoted
Scottish pupil and patron Jane Stirling;
her sister, Anne Houston, owned the
castle. Although suffering from
tuberculosis and bouts of depression,
he played a solo concert for two hours at
Edinburgh's Hopetoun Rooms and visited
other country houses belonging to the
sisters' relatives in Perthshire, Mid Calder
and Wishaw. He returned to Paris in
November and died of tuberculosis a
year later, aged just 39.

Rannoch Woods

Head back to Beith Road and to left, following a paved path to the left of the road and wall into Rannoch Wood, beautiful pocket of mixed woodland. After short distance, turn left at a waymark and follow a path to a junction. Keep right onto another path that sweeps left and rises through the woodland where there s lots of birdlife to spot, including chaffinch, great spotted woodpecker and chiffchaff. During late spring, there are a number of wildflowers, especially bluebells.

At a fork keep right, continue to a crossroads and keep straight on for Rannoch Road. At the next crossroads turn left for Elm Drive with the path now rising steadily through the wood. The path then levels off as it passes a children's play area to reach Elm Drive. Turn right out of Rannoch Wood and walk along Elm Drive but just before Rannoch Road turn left and follow a path into Bluebell Wood, the second pocket of woodland of this route.

The path initially runs parallel with Rannoch Road but shortly it crosses a footbridge over a burn with the path then rising gradually. When it splits keep right,

continue to climb to another fork and now go left before making the gentle descent to a T-junction. Keep right, drop down a flight of wooden steps and cross another footbridge. Soon afterwards bear right onto a path coming in from the left – signed for Elderslie – and follow this to a crossroads where you turn right.

After a few metres exit Bluebell Wood onto Castle Avenue and drop down to Auchenlodment Road. Turn left and drop downhill past Johnstone Burgh Football Club all the way to Beith Road. Turn right, walk along the pavement to Thornhill, go left and return to the station.

Kilbarchan

Distance 4.5km **Time** 1 hour 30
Terrain minor road, woodland and field
paths **Maps** OS Explorer 341 and 342
Access buses to Kilbarchan from Glasgow

**The charming village of Kilbarchan,
situated a few miles from Paisley, is
home to the Weaver's Cottage, which
provides a great insight into Kilbarchan's
weaving history. This walk follows local
paths and tracks to explore the
countryside surrounding the village.**

Begin from the war memorial near
the village centre at the corner of Churchill
Place and High Barholm. Head west along
High Barholm, then bear right onto Ewing
Street, which climbs to Steeple Street.
At the top it's worth turning right up steps
to explore Steeple Square, dominated by
the Kilbarchan Steeple.

Kilbarchan has two churches (its name
translates as the Place of St Berchan's

Church) but the Kilbarchan Steeple was
never a place of worship, instead it was a
combined school and market during the
18th century. Set within the steeple is a
bronze statue of Habbie Simpson (1550-
1620) who was the town piper. Inhabitants
of Kilbarchan are known as 'Habbies' in
his honour, and during the annual Lilias
Day celebrations it is customary for the
piper to 'come alive', the statue being
covered by a flag for the day.

At the bottom of Steeple Street bear
right and follow the pavement to Church
Street on the left. At its corner is the
Weaver's Cottage. Built in 1723 and cared
for by the National Trust for Scotland, the
cottage has period furniture in place, as
well as the last working handloom in
Kilbarchan (there were once more than
800 in the village) with the garden
growing plants that would have been
used to make fabric dyes.

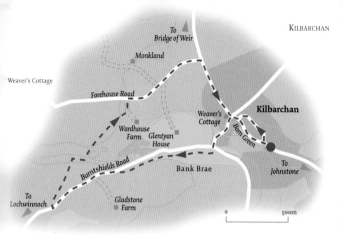

Many of the Kilbarchan weavers took art in a week of strikes and agitation which became known as the 'Radical War' April 1820. Harshly put down by the overnment, the leading Radicals were quickly rounded up and hanged, or sentenced to penal transportation.

Follow Church Street downhill past a ountain in memory of Robert Allan 774-1841), the Kilbarchan-born poet, eaver and friend of Robert Tannahill. t a T-junction cross Burntshields Road nto a woodland track, then after 10m urn right and follow a path gradually phill. After it steepens and curves harply left, continue on a gradual ascent, eering right to a fork. Go right and keep n beneath Bank Brae.

After approximately 300m, the path ears right and descends steeply to a ond. Turn left, follow it past the pond hrough the wood, eventually reaching urntshields Road. Turn left, follow the oad (watching for traffic) as it rises

gradually through lovely countryside for 350m, then turn right into a field at a public footpath sign for Dampton Pad. Head diagonally right across the field for 50m, cross a stone stile at the edge of a wall and bear right for a few metres before heading downhill through a gap in some gorse bushes. Beyond this, descend over the field and through an obvious gap in some hedges to a fence. At its right edge, cross a footbridge over a burn and follow the right edge of a field to the left of a wall, towards two electricity pylons.

After passing beneath the pylons, walk along the field edge beside a strip of woodland. At the edge of the wood, beside a red-brick building, cross a stone stile beside a public footpath sign. Turn left along a narrow road, then go right onto Forehouse Road and walk back to Locher Road in Kilbarchan. Turn right and head downhill into Kilbarchan along Shuttle Street and then Barn Green to return to the start.

Bridge of Weir and the Pow Burn

Distance 3.5km Time 1 hour
Terrain paths, pavement, minor road
Map OS Explorer 341 Access buses to
Bridge of Weir from Glasgow, Greenock
and Johnstone

Bridge of Weir developed around
the lands of the 15th-century Ranfurly
Castle. During the 18th-century cotton-
spinning was a major employer within
the village and there were a number of
mills here on the River Gryffe that cuts
its course through the town. This route
follows quiet roads as it explores Bridge
of Weir and Old Ranfurly with the route
bookended by a path through the
woodland that borders the Pow Burn.

The walk begins from Bridge of Weir's
bustling Main Street and its junction with
Torr Road. Follow Torr Road for 50m, then
turn left and climb a path to reach the

National Cycle Network Route 75 trail.
Turn left for Paisley and follow the path
which runs along the old Greenock and
Ayrshire Railway and the Bridge of Weir
Railway line, both of which closed in 1983
After heading southwest for 250m, you
reach the sculpture of an old train engine
Turn right, then left and walk down a
track past a cottage to a junction.

Head straight across the path, cross
a footbridge spanning the Pow Burn
and turn right. A path rises gently uphill
to the left of the burn, through lovely
peaceful woodland. This little glen has
lots of birdlife to see and hear during the
spring and summer months, including
brambling, blue tit and lesser redpoll.

Beyond the next footbridge climb a
stony path to cross the Pow Burn via
another footbridge. The path sweeps
left and rises gradually out of the

◀ Crossing the Pow Burn

woodland and into a small park. Carry on along a path as it climbs steps to gain a junction. Turn left, follow another path to the left of a wall and then exit the park onto Horsewood Road. Turn left and at a crossroads go straight across Prieston Road onto Lawmarnock Road which rises steadily alongside Old Ranfurly Golf Course.

In the grounds of the golf course, although somewhat hidden from view from the roadside, stands the remains of Ranfurly Castle, which was built in around 1440 by local landowners, the Knox family, ancestors of the religious reformer John Knox. It is thought the towerhouse was three storeys high but today its remains rise to about 7m.

Keep on along Lawmarnock Road to reach Kilgraston Road on the left. This quiet road runs between Old Ranfurly and Ranfurly Castle golf courses, with fine views across both. It is a lovely section of the route.

At Ranfurly Place go left and descend past Old Ranfurly Club House back to Prieston Road. Turn left, then after 100m turn right onto a track signed for Bridge of Weir

via The Glen. After passing a couple of houses the track ends. Now join a path that descends down a steep flight of steps into woodland. A path then leads back to the Pow Burn, which is crossed via a footbridge before continuing back into the park visited on the outward half of the walk. Turn right here and retrace your steps alongside the Pow Burn to return to Bridge of Weir.

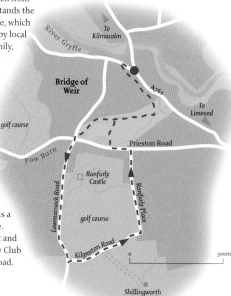

Bridge of Weir and the Gryffe

Distance 6.75km Time 2 hours
Terrain paths, pavement, minor road
Map OS Explorer 341 Access buses to
Bridge of Weir from Glasgow, Greenock
and Johnstone

Bridge of Weir was built on the manufacturing and spinning of cotton in the 18th and 19th centuries, and there is still visible evidence of the industry on this lovely walk which follows country roads and the River Gryffe.

Begin from Bridge of Weir's bustling Main Street and its junction with Torr Road. Follow Main Street southeast through the village for 200m, then turn left onto Mill Brae. Walk downhill and cross a bridge spanning the River Gryffe, which begins its journey nearby at Kilmacolm and flows for a further 24km into the Black Cart Water near Glasgow.

Once across the bridge turn right onto a wooded path that follows the fast-flowing river downstream – dipper and kingfisher may well be spied flitting along the surface. This attractive section of the route continues for around 200m, after which you bear right, down some steps, and continue along a riverbank path that can be a little rough underfoot. Wood sorrel and wood anemone flank the path during spring and summer.

The route improves underfoot as it passes an old weir before a raised path, known as the Mill Lade Path, heads through the woodland, making for easy walking. It's a peaceful section of the route through the Renfrewshire countryside, alongside a more languorous section of the river. The lade provided power for the Crosslee Cotton Mill, which was the biggest mill on the River Gryffe.

◀ River Gryffe

The mill opened in 1793 and in its heyday employed more than 300 workers. Velvet made at the mill was used on the seats in the House of Lords. Crosslee Mill was demolished in the early 20th century when the need for hand weaving declined.

Eventually the path forks beside an old bridge, known locally as the Fairy Bridge. Don't cross it; instead keep right for Crosslee and continue through the woodland to emerge onto Brierie Hill Road at the village of Crosslee. Keep right and follow the pavement uphill before it descends gently to reach the B789. Turn right, walk across a roadbridge spanning the River Gryffe and continue for nearly 200m before turning right onto Crosslee Road, signed for Bridge of Weir.

This scenic road heads southwest through charming countryside. In a while, where it splits, keep left to follow the road as it gently winds for another 500m to a bridge. Just before this, turn left up a path to reach the National Cycle Network Route 75 trail. Turn right and continue through the countryside as the cyclepath follows the lines of the former Greenock and Ayrshire Railway and the Bridge of Weir Railway lines.

After 1.25km the path passes under a roadbridge at Bridge of Weir Main Street. Continue for another 350m and turn right, beside a sculpture of an old train engine, descend through a car park to Main Street, turn left and return to the start.

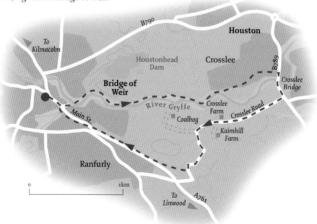

Houston and the Craigends Yew

Distance 8.5km Time 3 hours
Terrain paths, pavement, minor road
Map OS Explorer 341 Access buses to
Houston from Glasgow and Greenock

Houston is a quiet village surrounded by
attractive countryside. Lanes, paths and
minor roads circumnavigate the village
and visit a number of historic sites,
including the famous Craigends Yew.

Begin facing the 18th-century Mercat
Cross on South Street. Turn right, walk to
Bogstonhill Road and go left. After
crossing a bridge over the Houston Burn
go left onto North Street and pass a
number of attractive cottages to gain
Main Street. Turn right and walk away
from the village centre, passing its war
memorial. Carefully follow the roadside
verge through a scenic section of
Renfrewshire, passing Greenhill Farm
before turning right onto the narrow
Chapel Road.

After 175m, bear right and continue all
the way to Kirk Road. Turn left, pass
Houston and Killellan Kirk and continue
to a cottage called Lonend. Go straight
across the road to follow the narrow
Quarry Brae through another peaceful
part of the village. At a junction go right
and descend to Houston Road (B790).
Once across, keep left on a path, then left
again at a fork, following the path over
Leeburn Avenue and then Leeburn
Gardens into woodland.

The path winds its way to a track beside
Ardgryfe Crescent; there is a fine view
here along the River Gryffe. Turn right,
cross a bridge over the river, keep left at a
fork with the track, then a path,
proceeding through more woodland for
300m to an information panel.

Here you'll find the Craigends Yew,
thought to be Scotland's largest layering
yew (*Taxus baccata*). A layering yew is
formed when the branches of the parent

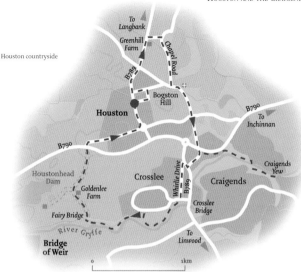

Houston countryside

tree grow in all directions, sweeping down to the ground before rising again to form a complete ring of new trees. The Craigends Yew grove is around 30m across and is thought to be at least 600 years old. In comparison, the famous Fortingall Yew in Perthshire is thought to be around 4500 years old, with a good claim to be the oldest living organism in Europe.

Retrace your steps all the way back to the B790. Cross Leeburn Avenue, then after 100m turn left and follow a lane to meet the B789. Turn right down steps just before it to go through an underpass, then climb the steps up the other side. Bear right onto Whirlie Road and follow this to a T-junction with Brierie Hill Road. Ahead is a small car park where

Crosslee Cotton Mill once stood. At the car park's right corner take a path that crosses down over grassland to the River Gryffe. The path sweeps right in a broad loop, but just before returning to Brierie Hill Road bear left onto the signed Gryffe Walkway. This is part of the mill lade path, the lade having once provided power for the Crosslee Cotton Mill. It heads through woodland for 700m to reach an old bridge, known locally as the Fairy Bridge.

Turn right over the bridge to follow a path rising to a road. Keep left and walk through countryside all the way to the B790. Turn left, then right onto Old Bridge of Weir Road to return to Houston. At a roundabout, turn left onto Main Street and descend back to South Street.

55

Knapps Loch

Distance 3.25km Time 1 hour 30
Terrain countryside paths and tracks
Map OS Explorer 341 Access no public
transport to the start

Knapps Loch sits on the outskirts of
Kilmacolm surrounded by woodland,
moorland and open countryside. Lots of
wildlife can be spotted and there are
great views. With small stands of trees
scattered around its edge, Knapps Loch
wouldn't look out of place in a Highland
setting but instead it nestles comfortably
at the eastern edge of Inverclyde. The
loch contains several small islands but is
actually man-made, created by a local
fishing club in the early 20th century.

There are two car parks that provide
access to Knapps Loch but for this route
the car park that sits 250m south of the
loch, beside the A761, is the start point.
From here cross a stile to the right of a
gate and climb a narrow grassy path
steadily east through mixed woodland.
It can be boggy but as height is gained
the route provides great views over
Knapps Loch. The path soon leaves the
woodland behind to head over open
moorland, crossing a broader grassy path.

As the gradient eases, with progress
made over some sections of slabby rock,
expansive views across the local
Renfrewshire and Inverclyde landscape
open out. Roe deer may well be spotted
within the heathery moorland, as well as
damselflies, dragonflies and butterflies
during summer.

Eventually, the path descends northeast

into a small pocket of pine woodland, which again can be muddy. It soon splits so keep right, cross a burn and exit the woodland where there is another superb view across Knapps Loch. On a clear day the distinctive outline of Ben Lomond and the distant mountains of the Southern Highlands are visible. The path drops steadily down to a gate. Once through, immediately take the right-hand of two gates and continue on a fairly steep descent, to the left of conifers, towards Knapps Loch.

When the gradient levels off, keep left at a crossroads, walk a few metres to a track, turn left again and now pass through

more woodland, all the way to another gate with more fine views. Beyond the gate, walk beside the loch's edge, crossing a field. Once over a footbridge spanning a burn, a firm track continues southwest near to the loch. It soon splits so keep left along a path, then step over a low wall.

Carry on along the lochside, crossing another low wall and enjoying birdlife such as mute swan, cormorant and great crested grebe out on the water. Pass through another gate, take a raised path above the loch and cross a bridge, then a stile in a wall near a boathouse. From the end of the loch, walk south away from the water, crossing a paved track and then a field as it rises gently, near to the A761. At the corner of the field, go through a gate and return to the start.

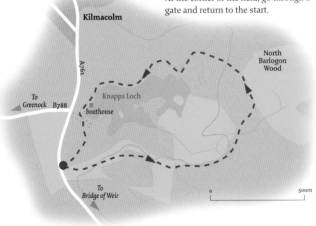

Quarriers Village and Kilmacolm

Distance 8.5km Time 3 hours
Terrain fields, paths and quiet roads
Map OS Explorer 341 Access bus to
Quarriers Village from Kilmacolm
and Johnstone

The peaceful village of Quarriers, which sits 15km west of Paisley, was established in 1878 as the Orphan Homes of Scotland charity. It was the idea of philanthropist William Quarrier, a devout Christian who was born a few miles away in Greenock in 1829 and rose from abject poverty to become a successful shoe retailer in Glasgow. In total, almost 40 cottages were built, along with a school and a church. Later a hospital was built, which treated more than 11,000 patients with tuberculosis between 1898 and 1948. Today Quarriers Village is still home to its social care headquarters and is a fascinating place for a wander.

From the small car park at the end of Faith Avenue, head southwest towards the village centre. The values of William Quarrier are reflected in the naming of the streets of the village, so as well as Faith Avenue you will find avenues of Love, Praise and Peace. You will also notice an unusual mix of architectural styles in the fine houses; Gothic, French, Old English, Scottish baronial and Italian all feature. Surprisingly, all were designed by the same architect, Robert Bryden, who worked – for free – on the village buildings over the course of 28 years.

At a junction, go right onto Church Road and follow this towards the imposing Gothic architecture of Mount Zion Church, adorned by a 36m-high steeple which can be seen for many miles around. Informally known as the Children's Cathedral when it opened in 1888, the church could hold a

Guardians of the path

ongregation of up to
000 and, over time, two
xtensions increased this
o 2000. Since its closure in
006, the church has been
onverted into private dwellings.

Facing away from the church,
ear right onto Love Avenue and
ontinue through Quarriers,
dmiring the intricate stonework
n many of the houses. Love
venue soon curves left to return to
aith Avenue where you go left and
walk back to the car park. Continue
hrough it, turning right after Somerville
Veir Hall. The first building to be
onstructed in the village, originally in
he style of a French chateau, this was
used as a school and church, as well
as initial living quarters for the
Quarrier family. Turn left downhill
and curve round on a rough road to
cross a bridge over the River Gryffe.

A paved path now winds its way
through open country with views
across Renfrewshire and Inverclyde,
rising gradually to reach the National
Cycle Network trail that runs between
Paisley and Gourock. Turn left onto this
for Kilmacolm and follow it northwest,
with views to Quarriers and Mount Zion
Church. Continuing, you pass the silent
Roman legion created for the cyclepath by
the artist David Kemp; keep an eye out for
buzzard and roe deer too.

In just under 3km, the path arrives at
Kilmacolm. After passing beneath a bridge
carrying Lochwinnoch Road, bear right
through a car park to reach Kilmacolm
village centre. The village dates back to
prehistoric times, but it really developed
with the arrival of the railway in 1869,
when many of the elegant Victorian and
Edwardian villas were built. Kilmacolm is
home to a number of fine cafés, perfect for
a pit stop before you retrace your steps to
Quarriers Village.

Kilmacolm and Glen Moss

Distance 4.75km **Time** 1 hour 30
Terrain minor road, paths
Map OS Explorer 341 **Access** buses to
Kilmacolm from Glasgow and Greenock

The Glen Moss Wildlife Reserve, on the
outskirts of the village of Kilmacolm, is
a little haven of peace and tranquillity.
The rich marshland, moorland and wet
heathland support a fantastic variety of
wildlife, and a network of firm paths
leads through the reserve.

From the corner of Lochwinnoch Road
and Bridge of Weir Road in Kilmacolm,
turn right onto Bridge of Weir Road, then
left onto Moss Road, which is followed
onto Gillburn Road. Where it splits, keep

right onto Gowkhouse Road, signed for
Glen Moss. This narrow road climbs uph
through two sets of gates, after which a
track rises gradually through woodland.
At a junction keep right, then after a few
metres go left into the reserve.

A path immediately splits. Keep right
and walk through the reserve, skirting
woodland to the right. Soon a section of
boardwalk continues, passing steps on
the right which are for the return journey
The boardwalk gives way to a path; keep
left when it splits before continuing
through the woodland in a clockwise
direction. A gradual climb reaches a
viewpoint where there is a sweeping
outlook across the reserve.

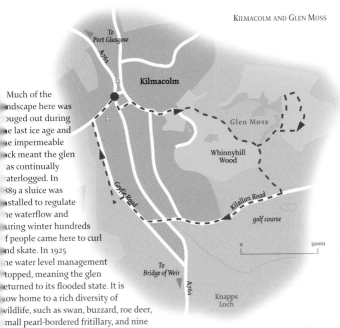

Much of the landscape here was gouged out during the last ice age and the impermeable rock meant the glen was continually waterlogged. In 1889 a sluice was installed to regulate the waterflow and during winter hundreds of people came here to curl and skate. In 1925 the water level management stopped, meaning the glen returned to its flooded state. It is now home to a rich diversity of wildlife, such as swan, buzzard, roe deer, small pearl-bordered fritillary, and nine species of damsel and dragonfly.

Follow the path over a short section of rocky slabs, then down some steps. Beyond a gap in a wall, the path curves right and passes through another wall. It continues across heathland filled with wildlife all the way back to the outward path. Turn left and return the way you came to climb the flight of steps on the left and reach the 8th tee of Kilmacolm Golf Course. Carry straight on along the edge of the course towards a strip of woodland, beside a low wall. The path bears right through a gap in the wall, then immediately turns left into the woodland and continues across the golf course to

emerge at Kilallan Road on the outskirts of Kilmacolm.

Turn right and follow this narrow road, which soon widens as it becomes Houston Road. As it descends there are extensive views across the countryside. At Bridge of Weir Road, go straight on to follow Houston Road downhill to Gryffe Road. Go right, walk through the leafy outskirts of Kilmacolm for 200m and then turn left onto a path that culminates at the National Cycle Network shared-use path. Turn right and continue back towards Kilmacolm. Once under a roadbridge spanning the path, walk through a car park to Lochwinnoch Road.

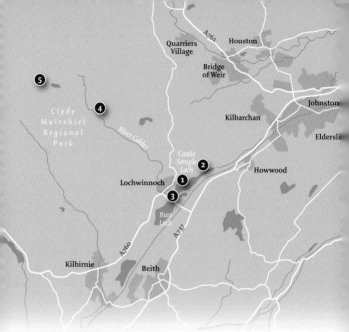

Clyde Muirshiel Regional Park straddles Renfrewshire and Inverclyde and offers a wealth of walking combined with a range of wildlife and extensive views to the mountains and out to sea.

The eastern side of Clyde Muirshiel Regional Park is dominated by Castle Semple Loch and the high ground of Muirshiel Country Park. The village of Lochwinnoch is a great base to explore everything Castle Semple has to offer, from a walk through Parkhill Wood to a wander along the banks of the loch or to the vantage point of Kenmure Hill. No matter which location you visit, there is plenty of wildlife to look out for, from

butterflies, damselflies and dragonflies on balmy summer days to great skeins of geese in the winter.

Heading uphill into Muirshiel Country Park, the summit of Windy Hill has panoramic views that you would little expect given the minimal exertion required to get here – the huge mountains of the Southern Highlands and the industrial sweep of Glasgow and Paisley are all visible on a clear day. Against this scenic backdrop is a walk out to the old barytes mine that was once crucial to the local economy. When here, you get a sense of the hardship the workers must have endured.

ochwinnoch and Muirshiel

Castle Semple Loch and Parkhill Wood

Distance 6.5km Time 2 hours
Terrain paths and tracks
Map OS Explorer 341 Access trains to
Lochwinnoch from Glasgow and Ayr;
buses to Lochwinnoch from Glasgow,
Irvine and Ardrossan

Castle Semple Loch, near the village of
Lochwinnoch, is a haven for wildlife
which thrives out on the water and in
the surrounding woodland. This walk
takes in the lochside and the adjacent
Parkhill Wood.

Lochwinnoch is well served by public
transport and Castle Semple Loch runs
along the eastern edge of the village.
There is a large car park and visitor centre
at Castle Semple Country Park. Walk east

through the car park but just before the
visitor centre turn left and climb a path to
gain the National Cycle Network trail. Go
right and follow the path, with views
across the loch, reaching a crossroads
after 1km. To the left is Parkhill Wood, but
carry straight on for another 1km to
Castle Semple Collegiate Church.

Bear left here onto a path (signed for
Parkhill Wood), descend through a gate,
then double-back left onto a track to reach
the remains of the church. Founded in
1504 by Sir John Sempill, the 1st Lord
Sempill, the church was intended to
house a college of clergy whose main job
was to pray for the souls of his family.
Sempill owned local estates and also built
a castle at the east end of the north shore
of what was then Loch Winnoch before he
was slain at the Battle of Flodden,
alongside most of Scotland's nobility.

The church was originally rectangular in
shape but was extended after Sempill's
death and was served by a senior priest, a
provost, six chaplains, two altar boys and

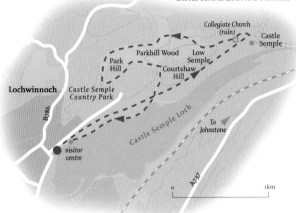

church officer. It was a place of worship until the Scottish Reformation and the break with Rome and the Papacy in 1560. Lord Sempill's ornate tomb is still on view in the north wall of the extension.

Continue along the track and beyond a gate enter Parkhill Wood, a beautiful slice of mixed woodland which is home to great spotted woodpecker, willow warbler, long-tailed tit and blackcap.

After the track passes between two gateposts, leave it by bearing right onto a path that crosses a burn to reach a crossroads. Carry straight on over another burn; the path now rises gently through Parkhill Wood, curving left to cross back over a burn via a footbridge. Here, turn right onto another path that, once over a footbridge, rises steadily, the woodland here home to some impressive gnarled trees. In a while, the path drops gradually to a junction. Keep to the right and go straight ahead, then shortly afterwards keep left at a fork for a steep climb above the treeline. At the top, the view extends across Castle Semple Loch and over the Renfrewshire countryside.

A fairly steep descent on steps leads back into the wood and all the way to a junction. Keep right, then right again and continue past a grotto, which would have been used by the Sempill family for picnics during the 18th century. Continue on the wooded path and, after crossing a footbridge over the Blackditch Burn, turn right at a junction. Descend gently beside the burn back to the outward path at the entrance to the wood. Go straight across the National Cycle Network trail and down a track to Castle Semple Loch.

Follow the shoreline where, depending on the season, tufted ducks, goldeneye, goosander, mute swans, black-headed gulls and greylag geese may be seen out on the loch. This takes you back past the visitor centre to the start.

◀ Castle Semple Collegiate Church

Kenmure Temple

Distance 7.75km **Time** 2 hours 30
Terrain paths and tracks, one short
section of pathless field
Map OS Explorer 341 **Access** trains to
Lochwinnoch from Glasgow and Ayr;
buses to Lochwinnoch from Glasgow,
Irvine and Ardrossan

Kenmure Temple is a familiar landmark
when exploring the Renfrewshire
countryside in and around Lochwinnoch.
Situated on top of Kenmure Hill, it was
built in 1760 for the McDowell family who
had taken ownership of Castle Semple
Estate from the impoverished Sempill
family in 1727. The folly remains in
remarkable condition and there are great
views from the hilltop.

Lochwinnoch is well served by public
transport and Castle Semple Loch runs
along the eastern edge of the village.
There is a large car park at Castle Semple
Country Park. Walk east through the car
park to pick up a lochside path, after
which a track continues with views of the
loch and its wildlife out on the water and
within the reeds and grasses. After 1km
the track sweeps left, just beside three
sculpted benches depicting some of the
wildlife to be spotted at Castle Semple.
At a crossroads, opposite the entrance of
Parkhill Wood, turn right and follow the
National Cycle Network trail east.

This allows easy progress through
lovely mixed woodland. Soon you'll pass a
path on the left near the remains of Castle

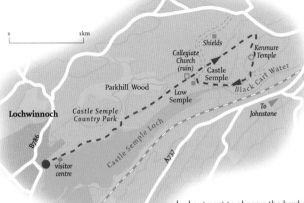

Semple Collegiate Church (this is part of your return route). The woodland now thins out with fine views of Renfrewshire opening up, particularly that of Kenmure Temple which can be seen on top of the craggy Kenmure Hill. Carry on to reach a path on the right, signed for Howwood.

Once through a gate, bear right and follow a field-edge path as it drops down and veers left to the base of Kenmure Hill where it broadens to a track. Here pick up a vague path on the left and follow it as it rises steeply to the summit with its terrific views along Castle Semple Loch, across the eastern fringes of Clyde Muirshiel Regional Park and out to Paisley, Glasgow and the Campsie Fells.

The exact purpose of the 'temple' on the summit is not known, although it is unlikely to have ever been used for anything religious. It may have been built as a lookout post to observe the herd of captive white deer on the estate during the 18th century and there is some evidence that 12 radiating avenues of trees were also planted down the hillside.

Take a southwesterly bearing and descend gradually over a field, cross a wooden bridge over a ditch, then turn right onto a track for Lochwinnoch. Follow this downhill for 350m but as it sweeps right keep straight on, cross a bridge over a burn that flows into the Black Cart Water and go through a gate. A grassy track leads near Castle Semple Loch to reach a gate at Low Semple Farm. Once through turn right, follow a farm access road to a junction, keep left, then at the next junction turn right. A track passes through a gate and under a bridge, after which bear left through a gate and follow a path back to the outward route.

Turn right and retrace your steps to the entrance of Parkhill Wood, turning left to return along the lochside to the start.

◀ Kenmure Temple

Lochwinnoch and Johnshill Loop

Distance 6.75km **Time** 2 hours
Terrain paths and tracks, pavement
Map OS Explorer 341 **Access** trains to
Lochwinnoch from Glasgow and Ayr;
buses to Lochwinnoch from Glasgow,
Irvine and Ardrossan

Lochwinnoch is set amongst the rolling
Renfrewshire countryside with Castle
Semple Loch extending from its eastern
edge. The RSPB also has a site at
Lochwinnoch with the loch and
surrounding woodland alive with flora
and fauna. A wander through Parkhill
Wood provides the opportunity to enjoy
the wildlife and local scenery.

Begin from Lochwinnoch Railway
Station, which sits on the outskirts of the
village. Carefully cross the A760 to the
entrance of the RSPB Nature Reserve
where, depending on the time of year,
grasshopper warbler, great crested grebe,

reed bunting, redwing, goldcrest, whooper
swan and kingfisher are prevalent.

To continue the walk, follow the path
that runs parallel with the A760, then
sweeps right to cross a footbridge
spanning the River Calder. Now the path
runs alongside Lochlip Road to the
entrance of Castle Semple Country Park.
Cross the entrance road to continue,
following St Winnoc Road into
Lochwinnoch village centre. Taking its
name from the 6th-century Saint Winnan
(who also gave his name to the Ayrshire
town of Kilwinning), Lochwinnoch
developed during the 12th century when
the monks of Paisley Abbey established a
church here. Industries such as
coalmining, thread manufacturing and
bleaching aided this development over
the centuries, as did the arrival of the
railway line in the 1840s.

At a junction go right onto Johnshill

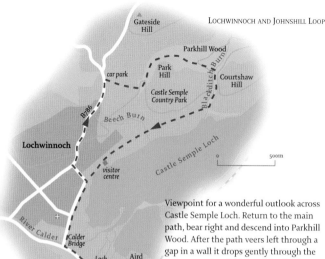

Gateside Hill

Parkhill Wood

Park Hill

Courtshaw Hill

car park

Castle Semple Country Park

Blackditch Burn

B786

Beech Burn

Lochwinnoch

Castle Semple Loch

visitor centre

0   500m

River Calder

Calder Bridge

Loch Bridge

Aird Meadow

Barr Loch

A760

Lochwinnoch Station

which climbs steadily past the remains of St John's Kirk; all that remains of this early 18th-century building is the impressive gable end plus belltower. Continue on the steady ascent for another 700m, then turn right through a car park, just before an electricity substation, into Castle Semple Country Park. Beyond a gate a path continues into Johnshill Field. During the summer months this is alive with meadow brown, ringlet and small tortoiseshell butterflies, damselflies and dragonflies.

After passing a magnificent old tree, the path splits. Take the right branch and walk the short distance to Johnshill

Viewpoint for a wonderful outlook across Castle Semple Loch. Return to the main path, bear right and descend into Parkhill Wood. After the path veers left through a gap in a wall it drops gently through the trees, sweeping right over a footbridge crossing a burn. Continue through the woodland all the way to a junction, looking and listening out for the birdlife, which includes great spotted woodpecker, willow warbler, blackcap and redwing, along the way.

Keep left and then, where it splits, go right for a stretch of easy walking. There are two paths on your right but continue going straight along the broad central track to the next junction. Go right here and shortly right again to accompany the Blackditch Burn all the way to a gate.

Exit Parkhill Wood through the gate and turn right onto the National Cycle Network trail. Follow this above Castle Semple Loch for 1km to a fork, where you keep left and drop downhill to the Castle Semple Country Park entrance beside St Winnoc Road. From here, retrace your steps to Lochwinnoch Railway Station.

◀ Castle Semple Loch

Windy Hill

Distance 2km Time 1 hour
Terrain woodland and hill paths
Map OS Explorer 341 Access no public
transport to the start

Clyde Muirshiel is Scotland's largest regional park and covers a huge area across Ayrshire, Inverclyde and Renfrewshire. A mixture of woodland, loch, coastline, moorland and hill supports lots of wildlife. Within its boundaries sits Muirshiel Country Park and one of its highest points is Windy Hill, which rises to 316m. Don't be put off by the height, however; this walk starts at 240m above sea level at Muirshiel Country Park Visitor Centre, so the short climb to the top along an excellent path is perfect for families.

Muirshiel Country Park Visitor Centre sits 7.5km northwest of Lochwinnoch at the end of a winding narrow road. Muirshiel Country Park opened in 1970 with the original woodlands and moorlands being managed in the late 1800s as a shooting estate. From the car park, walk to its more northerly exit and cross the road onto a path signed for Windy Hill. This firm path rises through lovely mixed woodland on a steady rise with fine views opening out west to Hill of Stake, the highest point of Clyde Muirshiel Regional Park.

The mixed woodland is soon replaced by denser sitka spruce and the incline increases here all the way to a junction. Sparrowhawks nest in the trees while fungi, which don't need a lot of light,

View from Windy Hill

thrive on the woodland floor. Turn left, then after around 30m keep right at a red waymark and continue uphill, with the path sweeping left and then right through a gap in a drystane dyke.

A scattering of trees, including birch and Scots pine, provide a more open landscape where black grouse are being encouraged to return. Roe deer may be spotted here too. Beyond a gate, the path now heads over open moorland with fine views across Muirshiel Country Park and the steep slopes of Windy Hill ahead. A mixture of path and boardwalk continues northeast, to the left of a drystane dyke, all the way to the base of Windy Hill.

Here the path splits into three. The left path is most direct, but also the steepest, so the centre path may be the best option as it climbs steadily,

curving left, to pick up the steeper route. It is then a sharp but short-lived ascent to the top of Windy Hill and its great panorama. To the north Ben Lomond and many of the Southern Highland peaks are etched on the horizon while the flatter plains of Renfrewshire extend to the east. A good portion of Clyde Muirshiel Regional Park is on show, as well as the urban sprawl of both Paisley and Glasgow on a clear day.

Carefully retrace your steps from the summit and continue all the way back to the visitor centre.

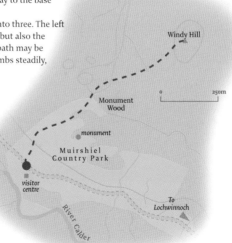

Windy Hill

Monument Wood

0 ———— 250m

● monument

M u i r s h i e l
C o u n t r y P a r k

● visitor centre

To Lochwinnoch

River Calder

Muirshiel Barytes Mines

Distance 8km Time 2 hours 30
Terrain moorland tracks
Map OS Explorer 341 Access no public
transport to the start

The high moorland that encompasses much of Muirshiel Country Park was, for many years, mined for the mineral barium sulphate, used in the production of paint, cosmetics, paper and porcelain. A firm track makes its way from Muirshiel Country Park Visitor Centre all the way to the old mineshafts.

Muirshiel Country Park Visitor Centre car park sits 7.5km northwest of Lochwinnoch at the end of a winding narrow road. Leaving the car park, turn left and follow the track northwest through a gate. From here the track makes its way across a wilder expanse of

moorland, home to lots of birdlife such a buzzard, kestrel, lapwing and skylark. It heads gently downhill, soon running above the early stages of the River Calder.

Ignore an old bridge spanning the river where you may spot the ruins of the mill, stables and former mineworkers' homes. Instead carry on for another 200m and veer left to cross another bridge over the Calder, signed for the Mine Track. When the barytes mineral was being mined it would have been transported along this track by horse and cart to the water-powered milling plant next to the River Calder. During the 20th century, motorised vehicles delivered the mineral to Lochwinnoch where it was then transferred to a plant in Glasgow.

At the end of the bridge, the track sweeps right and continues on a gentle

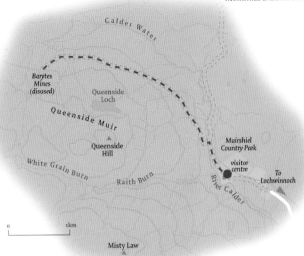

rise across the moorland near the west bank of the river. There are fine views of Windy Hill and the rocky spurs of Little Craig Minnan and Craig Minnan. As the walk proceeds, the outlook improves to take in large chunks of the rolling Renfrewshire countryside and, on a clear day, the distinctive outline of Ben Lomond and the twin peaks of Ben More and Stob Binnein beyond.

In a while, the track drops gently all the way to the base of the glen at which point it splits. Keep left and climb gradually to a small shelter. Beyond this, bear left onto a path for a short climb that leads above the site of the former mines – the area is now fenced in.

Barytes (barium sulphate) is a naturally occurring mineral and was mined at this site for around 200 years. From 1859 to 1920, production from open-cast gullies was low, with around 18,000 tons excavated during this spell. This increased considerably, however, when shafts were sunk to a depth of up to 200m in 1947, and by 1969, when production ceased, more than 274,000 tons of baryte had been brought to the surface. The mine provided employment for residents of Kilbirnie and Lochwinnoch, and by the early 1960s almost 50 people worked here.

This is a great spot for a break, with Ben Lomond still visible and the gorge of the Berryglen Burn, where barytes was excavated, now lined with birch and rowan. From here, retrace your steps to the start, with views across Renfrewshire, Glasgow and North Lanarkshire.

Port Glasgow, Greenock and Gourock
have a long tradition of welcoming
daytripping Glaswegians. There are still
plenty of busy ice-cream parlours, and
Gourock's fantastic open-air (but heated)
swimming pool is as popular as ever.

There are great coastal walks to be had
around here, whether this be to vantage
points such as Tower Hill and Lyle Hill or
long stretches of beach at Lunderston Bay
and the harbour at Inverkip – some lucky
wayfarers may spot porpoise, dolphin and
even orcas on their travels. However, as in
the previous chapter, the greatest variety

of routes is to be found within Clyde
Muirshiel Regional Park.

The centrepiece of this high moorland
plateau is the Greenock Cut, an
engineering marvel that makes for a
splendid walk. Just a little off the beaten
track are the Kelly Cut, the Wee Cut, Loch
Thom and Shielhill Glen SSSI, all offering
equally stunning walks.

Views that take in the contours of Arran,
the rugged sweep of the Arrochar Alps
and the long tapering line of the Firth of
Clyde also highlight why Inverclyde is
such a first-rate walking destination.

74

nverclyde

Finlaystone Country Estate

Distance 2.5km **Time** 1 hour
Terrain paths and tracks
Map OS Explorer 341 **Access** no public
transport to the start

Finlaystone Country Estate lies 5km east
of Port Glasgow and is a wonderful
sanctuary of woodland, waterfalls and
wildlife. The estate's history dates back
some 800 years and a castle was built
here during the late 14th century with
historical figures such as John Knox and
Robert Burns both staying at
Finlaystone. Today, at its centre, stands
the magnificent Finlaystone House,
which dates from the 18th century.

Finlaystone Estate has a café and gift
shop and there is an entrance charge.
Leaving the ticket office, turn right onto
the access road and, just after passing the
car park, turn left onto a path that crosses
a footbridge over the Finlaystone Burn.
Nearby is a waterfall – keep an eye out for
dipper along the river. A broad stony track
makes its way into lovely mixed
woodland. At a waymark turn right, then
immediately left and climb a steep path
through the woods.

Shortly afterwards, cross over a path and
bear left along a gently undulating trail,
passing through rhododendron bushes
that have formed themselves into tunnels
over the years. Beyond the
rhododendrons the path drops down to a
wall. Turn right here and continue
through the enchanting mature
woodland. At different times of the year
birdlife such as robin, blue tit, great tit,
long-tailed tit, blackbird, buzzard, jay,
kestrel, chaffinch, bullfinch, wagtail and
tree creeper may be seen and heard.

The path then descends to cross a

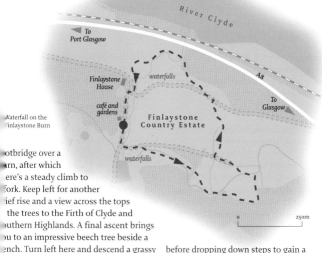

River Clyde

To
Port Glasgow

waterfalls

A8

Finlaystone
House

café and
gardens

To
Glasgow

Finlaystone
Country Estate

Waterfall on the
Finlaystone Burn

waterfalls

0   250m

otbridge over a
rn, after which
ere's a steady climb to
ork. Keep left for another
ief rise and a view across the tops
the trees to the Firth of Clyde and
uthern Highlands. A final ascent brings
u to an impressive beech tree beside a
ench. Turn left here and descend a grassy
th (which can be a little muddy) all the
ay to a junction. Keep left and continue
ownhill on a much firmer path to
nother footbridge spanning a burn.
Don't cross here; instead keep right and
escend, with the burn to your left, to
here the path splits. Take the left branch
ou'll hear the traffic rumbling along the
8 nearby) to the next fork. Keep right to
ain the access road for Finlaystone Estate
nd here turn left. After 50m, at a
aymark, turn right from the road onto a
ath that now meanders through the
oodland. Shortly afterwards, the path
weeps left down a flight of steps and
osses a wooden footbridge over
inlaystone Burn, which soon afterwards
ows into the River Clyde.

The path then continues past a waterfall
before dropping down steps to gain a
track. Turn left and follow it on a gradual
rise to gain the main access road next to a
lovely ornate bridge. Turn right and
follow the access road as it curves left,
with the imposing Finlaystone House
ahead. It is a striking building that was
extended by the architect Sir John James
Burnet in 1900; his other work included
Charing Cross Mansions and the Clyde
Navigation Trust building in Glasgow.

Robert Burns, whose patron was James
Cunningham, 14th Earl of Glencairn and
owner of Finlaystone, was a visitor to the
house and scratched his name on a
window pane. He also wrote a lament for
the earl, and named one of his sons James
Glencairn Burns in his benefactor's
honour. From here, it's a simple uphill
return to the start.

Greenock and Lyle Hill

Distance 6.5km Time 2 hours
Terrain pavement Map OS Explorer 341
Access trains to Greenock from Glasgow
and Gourock; buses to Greenock from
Glasgow and Largs

Greenock is the largest town in
Inverclyde, rising to prominence
through the refining of West Indian
sugar during the 18th century and then
shipbuilding. As Scotland's gateway to
the Triangular Trade in sugar, tobacco,
rum and sometimes people, Greenock
grew rich, and many of the buildings in
the town centre, particularly along the
Esplanade, reflect the prosperity that was
founded on ships, sugar and slavery. Lyle
Hill rises above the town and is home to
the Free French Memorial Cross,
dedicated to the memory of the French
seamen who perished in the Battle of the
Atlantic during the Second World War.

Begin from the eastern end of the
Esplanade, just beside Campbell Street
where there is ample parking. Head
northwest, with views across the Firth of

Clyde to the mountains at the edge of the
Southern Highlands. In summer, razorbill
guillemot, kittiwake and sandwich terns
are regular visitors, while porpoise and
even orcas have been seen out in the
water. As you walk, Rhu and the Cowal
Peninsula come into view and there is
lots of birdlife to spot out on the water.

After 1.75km, the Esplanade ends at
Eldon Street. Turn right, continue
alongside Battery Park and then turn left
onto Lyle Road, signposted for Lyle Hill.
Having crossed Newark Street, go under a
railway bridge beyond which Lyle Road
curves right and begins a sustained climb
It soon sweeps left, then right for fine

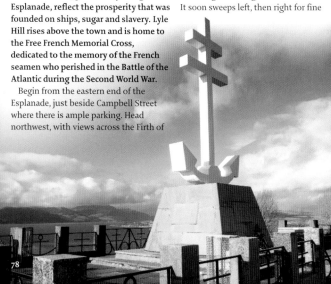

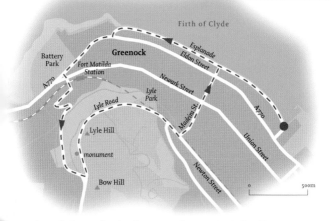

iews to Gourock. Eventually, after the
oad veers left twice more, a final short
se gains the Free French Memorial Cross.

The huge whitewashed Cross of
orraine combined with an anchor
epresents the Free French Naval Forces
ho based themselves in Greenock
hrough the Second World War. The Cross
f Lorraine was chosen by the French
esistance as a reply to the swastika
dopted by the Nazis. The base is made
rom granite and represents the enduring
trength of the 'Auld Alliance' between
cotland and France.

The natural harbour below, at Cardwell
ay, provided a safe haven for the
uilding and repairing of the Royal Navy
eet during the Napoleonic Wars while
hree of the great Cunard Liners – the
quitania, Queen Mary and Queen Elizabeth –
ere utilised as fast troop transporters,
ailing from here during the Second
orld War.

The summit of Lyle Hill sits a short
distance on. From here and from the Free
French Cross the outlook is stunning,
taking in much of the Inverclyde coast
and the Firth of Clyde, with Helensburgh,
Dunoon and Kilcreggan clearly visible on
its northern bank and Loch Long and Gare
Loch biting into the coast. Rising beyond
the water, Beinn Ruadh, on the Cowal
Peninsula, Beinn Chaorach (part of the
Luss Hills group) and The Cobbler are
prominent landmarks.

Turn back onto Lyle Road and begin the
gradual descent, enjoying the scenery.
Once past Lyle Park, with its view of
Greenock's skyline, including the striking
Victoria Tower, continue for another 300m
before turning left onto Madeira Street.
This drops all the way back to the
Esplanade where you turn right for a
short walk to the start, with views along
the Firth of Clyde to Dumbarton Rock, the
Kilpatrick Hills and the Erskine Bridge.

Free French Memorial Cross

Gourock and Tower Hill

Distance 4.75km Time 1 hour 30
Terrain pavement, paths
Map OS Explorer 341 Access trains to
Gourock from Glasgow; buses to Gourock
from Glasgow and Largs

**Gourock's position on the banks of
the Firth of Clyde makes it popular
with visitors and it is a great place for
a walk, with a variety of wildlife around
Cardwell Bay and some exceptional
views – one of the best vantage points is
Tower Hill.**

Battery Park sits near to Fort Matilda
Railway Station and has ample parking.
Battery Park is named because of the
coastal gun emplacement – or battery –
that was built to defend Greenock against
possible attack during the Napoleonic
Wars. Utilising spoil excavated from the
construction of the Greenock West to Fort
Matilda rail tunnel, Battery Park was also
a training ground for the Royal Scots
Fusiliers in the First World War and the
service area for Sunderland and Catalina
Flying Boats in the Second World War.

From the car park, follow the access
road northwest to reach the Firth of Clyde.
As the road sweeps left leave it for a path
that makes its way through the park and
along the coast – the views extend across
Gourock and over the Clyde to the
Southern Highlands. Tower Hill can also
be seen in the distance. Battery Park is a
wonderful place to view wildlife;
cormorant, oystercatcher, curlews,
porpoise, bottlenose dolphin and even
orcas may be seen at various times.

Continue through the park to a junction
and here turn right, following the path

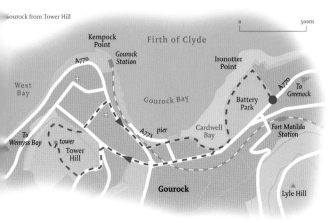

Gourock from Tower Hill

Firth of Clyde

Kempock Point

Gourock Station

A770

Ironotter Point

A770 To Greenock

West Bay

Gourock Bay

Battery Park

Fort Matilda Station

To Wemyss Bay

tower

A771

pier

Cardwell Bay

Tower Hill

Gourock

Lyle Hill

out of the park, then carry straight on to ardwell Road. Follow this to a roundabout and here take the second exit onto Broomberry Drive. A gentle climb takes you in 350m to Drumshantie Road on the left, signed for Tower Hill.

Almost immediately the road splits, so bear right onto Fletcher Avenue for a steep climb with fine views over the Firth of Clyde. Fletcher Avenue soon sweeps right and once across Darroch Drive you turn right and take a flight of steps onto a grassy track. This rises steadily but after the incline eases the path splits. Keep right for a gradual ascent to a small car park, beyond which is the summit of Tower Hill, adorned by a circular tower. The outlook is spectacular, taking in Gourock, the Firth of Clyde, Kilgreggan, Helensburgh, Dunoon, the Cowal

Peninsula and the craggy peaks of the Southern Highlands.

Descend back through the car park onto its access road, then turn right onto a paved path. This descends gradually through scattered woodland around the northern edge of Tower Hill, eventually dropping down a flight of steps. Follow these back to Broomberry Drive. Go straight across this onto John Street and walk downhill all the way to Shore Street.

Turn right and follow the pavement that runs parallel to the railway line. After some time, cross a bridge over the railway and follow a path over Chalmers Street to arrive at the shore on Tarbet Street. Cross the road, turn right and go round a barrier onto Cove Road, which extends above Cardwell Bay to Battery Park. It is now a short walk back to the start.

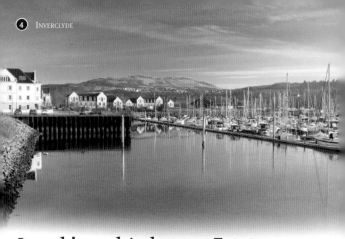

Inverkip and Ardgowan Estate

Distance 4.5km Time 1 hour 30
Terrain pavement, paths, minor roads
Map OS Explorer 341 Access trains to
Inverkip from Glasgow and Wemyss Bay;
bus to Inverkip from Greenock and Largs

**Kip Marina was the first marina in
Scotland when it opened in the early
1970s and remains one of the biggest in
Britain. Nearby Ardgowan Estate, on the
outskirts of Inverkip, is an historic area of
woodland and parkland, with paths and
tracks making for a fine family walk.**

From the main car park pick up a paved
path that runs past a play area and
between the marina and a restaurant. This
leads to Harbourside where you turn left
to continue around the marina to a
T-junction. Turn left here, then after just a
few metres go right onto the Clyde
Coastal Path, which quickly reaches the
coast. Turn right for Lunderston Bay,

following the path north around Inverkip
Bay with views to Arran and Cowal.

Enter Crowhill Wood, then after 75m
keep right at a fork and follow a path east
through the wood into Ardgowan Estate;
February sees a wonderful display of
snowdrops on the woodland floor. At a
junction go right and follow a track along
the southern fringes of the estate to a
three-way junction. Take the centre track
and continue through more lovely
woodland. As the track curves right keep
an eye out for Elizabeth's Grave, which
sits just left of the track under a canopy of
trees. It is a memorial for Elizabeth Sofia
Bulteel, the wife of Sir Guy Shaw Stewart
(1892-1976) who was 10th Baronet Shaw-
Stewart of Greenock and Blackhall and
Lord-Lieutenant of Renfrewshire.
This was her favourite walk. As the route
continues, the estate's old walled garden
can be seen to the right while high above,

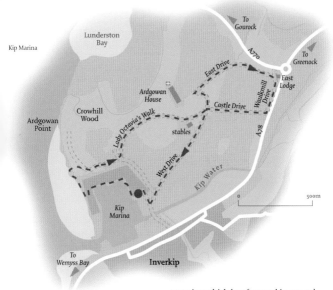

perched on top of the wooded slope, is the remains of the 15th-century Inverkip Castle. Soon afterwards, you pass the old stables, dating from 1801. The estate lands were gifted to John Stewart, the illegitimate son of King Robert III, in the early 15th century. Robert the Bruce fought twice at Ardgowan Estate, first on the side of the English in taking Inverkip Castle and then with the Scots when defending the castle.

At a crossroads keep left and follow West Drive as it rises gently and curves left to a gate. Once through this, you come to a junction. Ahead is Ardgowan House, a fabulous 18th-century Palladian mansion which has featured in several films and television dramas. The house also served as a hospital during both World Wars and had all its east-facing windows blown out by a bomb which fortunately missed the house during the Second World War.

Turn right here and descend East Drive through beautiful open grounds to East Lodge, then turn right onto Waulkmill Drive – named after waulking, a medieval process for thickening material. This briefly runs alongside the busy A78.

The route then veers right along Castle Drive back to West Drive near the stables. Go left and follow the access road through the estate to the marina.

Inverkip to Lunderston Bay

Distance 6.75km Time 2 hours
Terrain pavement, paths
Map OS Explorer 341
Access trains to Inverkip from Glasgow
and Wemyss Bay; buses to Inverkip from
Greenock and Largs

**This route follows a section of the Clyde
Coastal Path that runs from Kip Marina,
around Ardgowan Point, all the way to
Lunderston Bay, the closest sandy beach
to Glasgow and a popular destination for
families when the sun is shining.**

From the main car park, pick up a paved
path that runs past a play area and
between the marina and a restaurant. This
leads to Harbourside where you turn left
to continue around the marina to a
T-junction. Turn left here, then after just a
few metres go right onto the Clyde
Coastal Path, which quickly reaches the

coast. Turn right for Lunderston Bay,
following the path north around Inverkip
Bay with the outlook extending across the
Firth of Clyde to the Cowal Peninsula.

Enter Crowhill Wood, then after 75m
keep left at a fork and continue to hug the
coastline with the firm path providing
easy walking. Crowhill Wood is soon left
behind as the route now heads along a
rockier stretch of coast with fine views
extending to the craggy mountains of
the Southern Highlands and with open
countryside to the right. In a while the
path curves east and then north again
along the southern edge of Lunderston
Bay, which is part of Clyde Muirshiel
Regional Park.

Depending on the time of year,
oystercatcher, redshank, red-breasted
merganser red-throated diver, common
guillemot and great black-backed and

Lunderston Bay

black-headed gulls may be spotted out on the estuary and along the sandy and rocky shore. Grey seals and porpoise are also regular visitors.

Continuing north, the route is simple and leads all the way to the northern tip of Lunderston Bay where the sandy beach is extremely popular with visitors, especially when the weather is good. In the 1920s a tented village was set up during the summer months by families living in the nearby towns and villages who would spend their summer holiday here. Lunderston Bay was also used as a tented village for soldiers wounded in the First World War. As well as the tents and chalets, the camp included a first aid station, grocery shop, chip shop and baker's, with games and social events organised. The tradition of tented villages ceased with the onset of the Second World War.

To return to Kip Marina simply retrace your steps along the outward route, with views of Toward Point and across Bute to Arran's serrated profile.

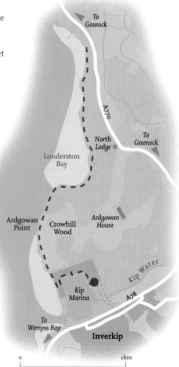

Shielhill Glen Nature Trail

Distance 2.75km Time 1 hour
Terrain paths Map OS Explorer 341
Access no public transport to the start

**Clyde Muirshiel Regional Park includes
the high ground above Greenock and
Gourock and offers a variety of walking
routes, including this little gem through
Shielhill Glen. Starting from the
Greenock Cut Visitor Centre, an excellent
path drops down through broadleaf
woodland before rising up to cross the
heathery moorland.**

The visitor centre has a large car park
and toilets while adjacent, at the
Ardgowan Fishery, is a café which is
perfect for post-walk refreshments. Exit
the car park and turn right, crossing the
road at the junction onto a path that runs
briefly above the north side of the Kip

Water. To the right is a memorial to
Robert Thom (1774-1847), the civil and
hydraulic engineer who designed the
Greenock Cut in the 1820s, a novel water
supply for the expanding town which
involved the construction of holding
reservoirs and an aqueduct which
conducted water in cascading races to
power numerous mills.

The path quickly drops down through a
gate and crosses a footbridge to continue
southwest along the Greenock Cut in a
corridor of mixed woodland. After 600m
go through a gate, then bear left onto a
path signed for the Nature Trail. Before
turning, take a moment to enjoy the view
that extends across the Firth of Clyde to
the Cowal Peninsula.

Wintering barnacle geese may be
spotted in the fields here. Walk down

Shielhill Glen

steps and pass through a gate from which a gradual descent takes you into the stunning wooded Shielhill Glen and all the way down to the glen floor; this is a beautiful secluded section of the route.

The woodland is designated as a Site of Special Scientific Interest due to the silver birch, oak, ash and rowan trees, many of them cloaked in moss and lichen. Continue to the right of the Kip Water before a section of boardwalk crosses the river. It is crossed two more times before the boardwalk reaches a gate. Once through, the boardwalk sweeps away from the Kip Water and begins a gradual ascent up a series of steps, leading above the

treeline and onto heather-clad moorland. Skylark, lapwing and even hen harrier may be spotted on the moorland and there are good views onto Dunrod Hill.

The climb continues, eventually rising to reach the Kelly Cut, which was built in 1845 to supplement the water supply to the Greenock Cut. From this high moorland vantage point there is a mesmerising view across Clyde Muirshiel Regional Park all the way to the Arrochar Alps. Turn left and follow the firm track of the Kelly Cut, which continues northeast for nearly 1km, passing through a gate to reach a road. Turn left and walk the short distance back to the visitor centre.

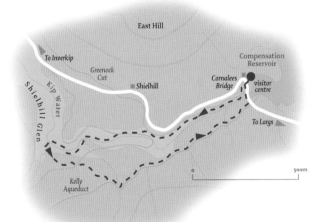

East Hill

To Inverkip

Greenock Cut

Shielhill

Kip Water

Shielhill Glen

Compensation Reservoir

Cornalees Bridge

visitor centre

To Largs

Kelly Aqueduct

0   500m

The Greenock Cut

Distance 11.5km Time 3 hours
Terrain paths and tracks
Map OS Explorer 341 Access no public
transport to the start

Designed by the Ayrshire-born Robert
Thom, the Greenock Cut was built
between 1825 and 1827 to carry water
from higher reservoirs down to Greenock
to power the thirsty cottonmills during
the town's industrial heyday.

Greenock Cut Visitor Centre sits 6km
above Greenock. There is a large car park
and toilets while adjacent, at the
Ardgowan Fishery, is an excellent café.
Exit the car park and turn right, crossing
the road at the junction onto a path
beside the Kip Water. This shortly goes
through a gate and crosses a footbridge to
now follow the Greenock Cut through a
peaceful landscape. Beyond another gate

where the path splits, keep right and
continue past Shielhill Farm.

Pass through two gates, on either side
of a single-track road, after which an
excellent path crosses the moorland of
Clyde Muirshiel Regional Park, still
following the Cut, with views of the River
Clyde and the Southern Highlands. Along
the way, the path passes a number of old
stone bridges – there are 23 in total – as
well as two stone bothies built as basic
workers' accommodation during
construction of the Cut.

Creating the Cut wasn't without
its problems, and in November 1835,
40 people tragically drowned when one
of the main dams collapsed and the east
end of Greenock flooded. A tunnel now
carries the water to Greenock with
the Cut recognised as a Scheduled
Ancient Monument.

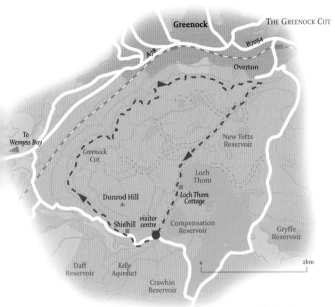

The route continues, with the view extending southwest across the Firth of Clyde towards Arran and north to the jagged peaks of the Arrochar Alps on the horizon. In a while, the path veers right above a steep gorge, crosses a bridge beside a lovely waterfall and then sweeps left before snaking its way across the moorland. Keep an eye out for buzzard, sparrowhawk, hen harrier and skylark.

Once across another stone bridge, a grassy path cuts through birch, rowan and hawthorn woodland. Beyond this, the church spires and industrial cranes at Greenock are prominent from this height and the track continues all the way to a cottage at Overton. However, just before the cottage turn right, cross a bridge and go through a gate onto the broad Overton Track, which climbs gently southwest away from Overton, passing a small reservoir. On reaching a fork, take the right track to pass another reservoir, then go through a gate.

A steady rise leads past the wonderfully named Scroggy Bank: when the track splits here, go left for a gentle descent past Loch Thom, a tranquil spot for viewing the wilder aspects of Clyde Muirshiel Regional Park. Carry on along the Overton Track, passing lonely Loch Thom Cottage, with the final stretch leading past Compensation Reservoir.

At the end of the track go past the fishery café, then through a gate beside a cattle grid to return to the visitor centre.

◀ Firth of Clyde from the Greenock Cut

The Wee Cut

Distance 7.5km Time 2 hours
Terrain paths and tracks
Map OS Explorer 341 Access no public transport to the start

The Greenock Cut gets all the plaudits as a walk; however, a route around the Wee Cut crosses a wild expanse of moorland with spectacular views, as well as visiting three smaller reservoirs that were vital for Thom's grand scheme for Greenock.

Greenock Cut Visitor Centre has a large car park and toilets, while there is an excellent café at the adjacent Ardgowan Fishery. Exit left from the car park onto a minor road (known as the Overton Track), go through a gate beside a cattle grid and walk past the café. Continue northeast past Compensation Reservoir, taking in views of Dunrod Hill. This reservoir was built in the 1820s as part of Robert Thom's hydro scheme, taking water from Loch Thom and storing it before it flowed down the Cut into Greenock.

Beyond Compensation Reservoir, the road rises gradually past Loch Thom and Loch Thom Cottage; as the track sweeps right there is a good view across the loch. Keep on for another 1km and, just as the track begins to descend beneath White Hill, bear left at a junction onto an access road signed for Dunrod Hill. After a steady rise, the incline eases with views opening out across Clyde Muirshiel Regional Park. As you approach two radio masts, further extensive views are revealed and at the highest point of the route (277m above sea level) the outlook extends to Greenock, the Firth of Clyde, the towns and villages along the Clyde coast and the big hills of the Southern Highlands.

Ignore a track on the left for Dunrod Hill

Firth of Clyde from the Wee Cut

here; instead keep to the access road as it passes the masts and then descends a stony track northwest towards No 3 reservoir, with a view of the Luss Hills. Just before the dam wall, at its eastern tip, bear right onto a rough track which drops easily down to pick up the Wee Cut. Turn right and follow the grassy path northeast, to the left of the aqueduct that links Nos 3, 4 and 5 Reservoirs. They were known as Balancing Reservoirs which allowed the water levels of the Greenock Cut to be maintained.

Follow the path across the moorland to pass No 4 Reservoir, as well as a bridge and a stone building, evidence of some of the infrastructure that was in place when the aqueduct was in use. Upon reaching No 5 Reservoir take the small stone bridge across the Wee Cut, turn left and follow a grassy track near the banks of the reservoir, culminating

at a stony track. Turn right for a gradual climb all the way to join the Overton Track. Go right, taking in the view before you do so, after which a steady rise returns to the outward track beneath White Hill. It is then a simple return beside Loch Thom and the Compensation Reservoir to the visitor centre.

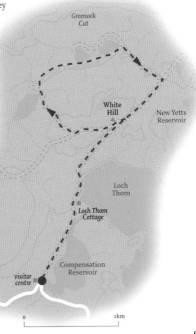

Loch Thom via Old Largs Road

Distance 8.75km **Time** 3 hours
Terrain paths, tracks and minor roads
Map OS Explorer 341 **Access** no public
transport to the start

Loch Thom, Compensation Reservoir
and Gryffe Reservoir all nestle within the
high ground of Clyde Muirshiel Regional
Park. A path along the northern edge of
Loch Thom, combined with tracks and
the minor road, makes for a fine walk
with great views and lots of birdlife.

The start point is Greenock Cut Visitor
Centre. Turn left from the car park onto a
minor road and beyond a gate, beside a
cattle grid, follow the Overton Track past
the Ardgowan Fishery and its café. After
passing Compensation Reservoir, the
track rises gradually all the way to Loch
Thom Cottage. Walk for another 500m,
then turn right onto a path signed for Old
Largs Road.

Descend steadily east to reach Loch
Thom where a grassy path – which can be
muddy at points – continues alongside
the loch. Flocks of Canada, Brent and
barnacle geese can be seen and heard out
on the water during the winter months
with curlew, oystercatcher and
greenshank just a few of the summer
visitors. The path undulates gently, soon
picking up an old rough road (which is
traffic free). As height is gained above
Loch Thom, views extend over the
moorland of Clyde Muirshiel Regional
Park, and you get a sense of the size of
Loch Thom from here.

When built in 1827 by the Shaws Water
Company, it was known as the Great
Reservoir (with a capacity to hold 1800
million gallons of water) and was only
later named Loch Thom after Robert
Thom, the Scottish engineer who
designed the Greenock Cut aqueduct to

Loch Thom

carry water from Compensation Reservoir and Loch Thom to the mills of Greenock. The road then curves left away from Loch Thom before dropping gently across the moorland with Corlic Hill and its radio mast coming into view. After passing through a gate, the road rises steadily to gain Old Largs Road, a scenic route that crosses the high moorland between Greenock and Largs. Turn right and, keeping an eye out for traffic, follow it south, with cattle and sheep usually grazing near the verge and a lovely outlook across both Gryffe Reservoir and Loch Thom.

After passing through a gate beside a cattle grid, you can turn left from the road and follow a track a short distance to reach the peaceful Gryffe Reservoir, a fine spot for a break. As with Loch Thom, the two reservoirs of Gryffe were built to carry clean water for several miles, via a tunnel, down to Greenock.

Return to Old Largs Road and continue along the shore of Loch Thom. Follow the road as it then sweeps right and continues for another

1.5km before turning right onto a narrow road at the head of Loch Thom, signed for Greenock Cut Centre. After passing through a gate beside a cattle grid, cross a bridge to follow the road along Loch Thom's western edge. In time, the road descends, with Compensation Reservoir coming back into view as you return to the visitor centre.

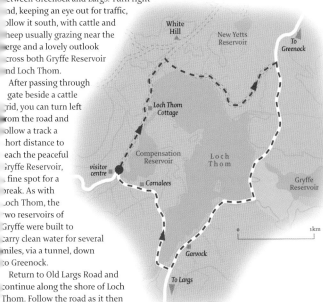

The Kelly Cut

Distance 12km Time 4 hours (round trip)
Terrain paths and tracks
Map OS Explorer 341 Access no public
transport to the start

Sitting around 200m above sea level, the Kelly Cut was built in 1845 to supplement the water supply to the Greenock Cut. It is less well known than its more popular neighbour but that doesn't mean it is not worth exploring. This out-and-back walk crosses a wilder section of moorland, known as the Leap Moor, with great views and plenty of interesting wildlife.

The start point of the route is Greenock Cut Visitor Centre. Exit right from the car park to a junction and keep left, crossing the roadbridges that span the early stages of the Kip Water and the outflow from the adjacent Compensation Reservoir. Shortly afterwards go right through a gate signposted for the Kelly Cut. A good track which can be boggy at times, leads you southwest across Leap Moor, a broad expanse of peat moorland, a massive carbon store that sits on top of an ancient lava flow, which is up to 1km thick.

Continue above Shielhill Glen, an area of woodland that drops west away from the Kelly Cut, with the track winding southwest under the slopes of Crawhin Hill. Birdlife to look out for around here includes lapwing, skylark, wheatear, curlew and hen harrier while foxglove, buttercup, bogcotton, sundew and butterwort are some of the wildflowers to be found. Rowan and alder trees line the path. As progress is made, views open out across the irregular outline of Daff Reservoir and to Leapmoor Forest, while further on spectacular views extend over

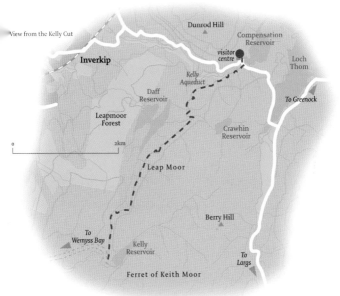

View from the Kelly Cut

Dunrod Hill

Compensation Reservoir

visitor centre

Loch Thom

Inverkip

Kelly Aqueduct

To Greenock

Daff Reservoir

Leapmoor Forest

Crawhin Reservoir

0   2km

Leap Moor

Berry Hill

To Wemyss Bay

Kelly Reservoir

To Largs

Ferret of Keith Moor

the Firth of Clyde to the Arrochar Alps.

After 2km the track veers sharply to the left to cross a wooden bridge where there are a couple of old bits of machinery once used to control the waterflow along the Kelly Cut. It then continues southwest with the scenery now stretching to the rugged mountains of the Southern Highlands. Beyond Daff Reservoir the route has a wilder air as it is surrounded by moorland and rounded hills, such as Wenchly Top.

Soon afterwards a footbridge takes the track across a burn flowing from the Kelly Cut with the track now continuing south, eventually culminating at an access track

for the Kelly Reservoir, which can be followed left up to reach the dam. It is a great place for a break with views across the Firth of Clyde to Toward Point and its whitewashed lighthouse, the Isle of Bute and the incredible outline of Arran. To return to the visitor centre it is then a matter of retracing your steps.

The inward return of the route is perhaps even better than the outward half as the track provides great views of Dunrod Hill's shapely outline, although it will be the Arrochar Alps that fill the horizon, particularly Beinn Ime, Beinn Narnain and The Cobbler; on a clear day Ben Lui is also visible.

Index